CW00418284

known and loved R. T. Kendall for over four decades, and in the multitude of books that have flowed from his prolific pen, he has never been more spot-on. Read it, and you will never have to ask again…Whatever happened to the Gospel?

—O. S. HAWKINS
FORMER PASTOR, FIRST BAPTIST CHURCH, DALLAS, TEXAS;
AUTHOR, THE CODE SERIES

R. T. Kendall has done it again. He has written an important book addressing one of the most important truths for this hour in his new book, *Whatever Happened to the Gospel?* This book is long overdue. It is more than relevant; it is critical. Its message is desperately needed in this hour. RT boldly, yet clearly, addresses many important truths, including one of the great errors being promoted today—the hyper-grace message. He addresses it with biblical precision, practical application, and prophetic urgency. I find it appropriate that this book is being published at Martin Luther's five hundredth anniversary—we need to return to proclaim the true Gospel of Jesus Christ. R. T. Kendall is a rare and precious gift to this generation.

—MIKE BICKLE
INTERNATIONAL HOUSE OF PRAYER OF KANSAS CITY

I love the title of this brilliant new book, written by my good friend Dr. R. T. Kendall. It's a vital question for such a time as this. Some parts of this book will likely stretch and challenge you; other moments will inform and inspire. But the common thread found on every single page is RT's passion to pursue the Gospel, the whole Gospel, and nothing but the Gospel.

—MATT REDMAN
SONGWRITER

With all the disquieting messages of today, how do we discern the Gospel of Jesus Christ? Fortunately we have R. T. Kendall, our tireless, truth-telling friend who speaks personally, historically, and clearly to proclaim God as He is. In listening to the practical teaching in this book, we settle on the main news of life; it is not heavy news, not sad news, but good news. For me, my family, and my patients, it is news too good to be true!

—ANDERSON SPICKARD III, M.D., M.S.
ASSISTANT DEAN, VANDERBILT UNIVERSITY
SCHOOL OF MEDICINE

This book is a spiritual shot of adrenaline to a church that is in cardiac arrest. It will be seen as controversial by many, but that itself tells us something of the malaise that we find ourselves in within evangelicalism. Love it or loathe it, we cannot and we must not ignore what RT has written. The spiritual health of God's people is at stake.

—MALCOLM DUNCAN
SENIOR PASTOR, GOLD HILL BAPTIST CHURCH, UK;
THEOLOGIAN; AUTHOR; BROADCASTER

Courageous, convincing, and uncompromising—a voice that needs to be heard. *Whatever Happened to the Gospel?* may prove to be R. T. Kendall's lasting legacy—a prophetic and clarion call to return to the biblical Gospel.

—GREG DOWNES
DIRECTOR, MINISTERIAL TRAINING, WYCLIFFE HALL,
OXFORD

RT is right on point. For example, when have you heard a teaching or even a mention of the power in the precious blood of Jesus? The only way this generation won't be deceived as

Jesus warned us is to read, study, and pray His Word! Thank you, RT, for being a voice in the wilderness.

—RICKY SKAGGS

COUNTRY MUSIC RECORDING ARTIST

I thank God for my friend R. T. Kendall and his thought-provoking book *Whatever Happened to the Gospel?* As missionaries giving our lives for the last thirty-seven years, we have watched so many come to salvation through the cross. We have also sadly seen many who have begun to slip away from the Gospel into a weak universalist theology. RT has written a clear, direct, to-the-point explanation of the plain, pure Gospel of salvation in Jesus Christ, which Rolland and I have given our lives to minister. In these days when so much is emphasized in the church at the expense of the Gospel, it is a joyous relief to again be centered on the goal of our faith, the salvation of our souls! RT places our confidence entirely in Jesus and the power of the cross, and for that reason this book is welcome and desperately needed.

—HEIDI BAKER

IRIS GLOBAL

There simply is not anything more important than the salvation of our souls. Finally in R. T. Kendall's latest book, *Whatever Happened to the Gospel?*, we are redirected to the greatest issue of our lives: Are we saved? In a time when nearly everything else in the Christian life is being trumpeted from pulpits, RT ministers rock-solid confidence in Jesus and the cross for our eternal hope. Let no other perspective undercut your peace and security. Let this book help you focus your faith squarely and precisely on what brings everlasting life and all that salvation means in Jesus!

—ROLLAND BAKER

IRIS GLOBAL

As I read every word in this book, *Whatever Happened to the Gospel?*, I was thinking, "What does Jesus think about what is said?" After all, the Father had this in mind when Jesus came and died on the cross and said, "This Gospel must be preached in all the world." The Holy Spirit empowers the followers of Jesus to preach the Gospel. I am totally convinced that this is the true message from the heart of God. Simple in calling people to Jesus to be saved yet solid in theology. I am so blessed that my dear friend and brother Dr. Kendall has taken the bold step to write this timely book. I fully endorse this profound message. May we all share the true message of the Gospel of Jesus with all the world.

A pilgrim follower of Jesus,

—ARTHUR BLESSITT
LUKE 18:1

R. T. Kendall has written dozens of great books that I have deeply appreciated, but *Whatever Happened to the Gospel?* is his crowning achievement. This is Luther's Ninety-Five Theses, except it is nailed to the very heart of every true Bible-believing Christian. Never in modern history has the Gospel of Jesus been in such great peril from so many fronts. *Whatever Happened to the Gospel?* clears away all of the sludge that has been added to the Gospel of late. This is a must-read for every truly concerned believer.

—MICHAEL YOUSSEF, PHD
VICAR, CHURCH OF THE APOSTLES, ATLANTA;
AUTHOR, BEST-SELLING *THE BARBARIANS ARE HERE*

A powerful, prophetic trumpet blast and clarion call to return to and remain in the greatest news the world has ever known: the Gospel that Jesus and His disciples taught. Read and rejoice in the Great Reformation truths expounded in this persuasive book, for herein lies our hope: first and foremost, the Gospel is the power of God for salvation.

—HOWARD SATTERTHWAITE
LEAD ELDER, WESTMINSTER CHAPEL, LONDON

It is hard to exaggerate the importance of this intensely personal, deeply theological, and absolutely relevant book. It's back to the Gospel, or we're going nowhere. The recovery of the historic message of Jesus, Paul, and all the New Testament apostles is the only thing that will keep this generation from sinking deeper and deeper into atheism, false religion, and despair. I urge every Christian, church leader, and sincere seeker to read this book.

—REV. COLIN DYE
SENIOR MINISTER, KENSINGTON TEMPLE, LONDON

In the 1960s the rise of a more charismatic emphasis within the evangelical movement led to worldwide blessing. But now many parts of the evangelical world are wandering away from the Gospel in a manner that is alarming, to say the least. RT's analysis and warnings deserve careful attention, and his remedy is obviously the right one—back to the Gospel!

—MICHAEL EATON, PHD (1942–2017)
(ONE OF MY DEAREST AND CLOSEST FRIENDS,
MICHAEL, WHO LIVED IN NAIROBI, KENYA,
WROTE THIS ENDORSEMENT ONLY DAYS BEFORE
HE DIED IN JOHANNESBURG, SOUTH AFRICA,
WHILE AT A CONFERENCE WITH ME.)

We know RT as a Bible teacher. This book is RT the prophet speaking the word of the Lord with unyielding biblical thoroughness into the life and witness of the church in our times. In the secular world we attach the word *prophet* to something new and innovative. In the Bible prophets more often than not called God's people back to things that had been forgotten. That is what this book does. It is alarming that it is needed, for it is nothing short of a recall to the Gospel itself, which RT believes several hugely popular erroneous trends in the evangelical and charismatic church are obscuring. For what it is worth, as a leader for many years in the charismatic wing of the church I agree with him. It is fitting that in 2017, the year that marks the five-hundredth anniversary of Luther's nailing his Ninety-Five Theses to the church door in Wittenberg, such a clarion call is being raised. Will it be listened to or dismissed? Scripture sadly tells us that either reaction is possible from God's people to the voice of a true prophet.

—REV. KENNY BORTHWICK
CHURCH OF SCOTLAND MINISTER; FORMER LEADER,
CLAN GATHERING AND NEW WINE SCOTLAND

I want to recommend *Whatever Happened to the Gospel?* to all who are hungry to follow truth. We will never accomplish our mission of John 17:17 without truth. This book will cause us to take a closer look at what is being preached and why.

—BOBBY CONNER
EAGLES VIEW MINISTRY

With accessible wisdom and masterful insights, RT contends for the true and authentic Gospel. Debunking all bold and subtle errors, whether they be from knowledgeable sources, misguided charlatans, or theological naïveté, this book is a plea and a clarion call to the church to get back to the Gospel that was given to us in all its full-orbed beauty, sufficiency, and power.

—TOPE KOLEOSO
JUBILEE CHURCH, LONDON

R. T. Kendall's ministry, both at Westminster Chapel, London, and now in the wider world, has significantly impacted those of us who cherish both Word and Spirit for life transformation. RT has never been afraid of controversy for the sake of truth and life, so here he draws the line from the Reformation to today and reminds us how easy it is to lose the Gospel of faith alone, grace alone. This passion for the Gospel and the Spirit needs to move us too.

—ROGER WELCH
LIFE IN THE SPIRIT TEAM, UK;
FORMER CHAIR, WYCLIFFE GLOBAL ALLIANCE

WHATEVER
HAPPENED
TO THE
GOSPEL?

WHATEVER HAPPENED

TO THE

GOSPEL?

R. T. KENDALL

CHARISMA
HOUSE

Most Charisma House Book Group products are available at special quantity discounts for bulk purchase for sales promotions, premiums, fund-raising, and educational needs. For details, write Charisma House Book Group, 600 Rinehart Road, Lake Mary, Florida 32746, or telephone (407) 333-0600.

Whatever Happened to the Gospel? by R. T. Kendall
Published by Charisma House
Charisma Media/Charisma House Book Group
600 Rinehart Road
Lake Mary, Florida 32746
www.charismahouse.com

Cover design by Lisa Rae McClure
Design Director: Justin Evans

Visit the author's website at https://rtkendallministries.com/.

Library of Congress Cataloging-in-Publication Data:
An application to register this book for cataloging has been
submitted to the Library of Congress.
International Standard Book Number: 978-1-62999-471-0
E-book ISBN: 978-1-62999-472-7

While the author has made every effort to provide accurate
telephone numbers and internet addresses at the time of
publication, neither the publisher nor the author assumes
any responsibility for errors or for changes that occur after
publication.

18 19 20 21 22 — 987654321
Printed in the United States of America

To every person who upholds and
preaches the Gospel of Christ.

If you read history, you will find that the Christians who did most for the present world were precisely those who thought most of the next! It is since Christians have largely ceased to think of the other world that they have become so ineffective in this.

—C. S. Lewis[1]

CONTENTS

FOREWORD

EAVEN IS REAL, friends, and yes, Hell is also real! It is clearly taught by Jesus and in many scriptures. R. T. Kendall, in his latest and very timely book, *Whatever Happened to the Gospel?*, could not bring these truths and corrections to us more clearly or more powerfully. RT makes the point that this is the primary reason Christ came to the earth: to save us from the coming judgment at the end of life on the earth and to give us an opportunity to miss Hell and gain Heaven for eternity.

Jesus came to rescue you. He came to save you from certain judgment from the perfect One, God, your Creator. He is perfect in every way and therefore cannot allow injustices to remain outstanding. The debt must be paid. This was God's dilemma. The human race that He so loves is incapable of living unselfishly, without getting hurt or hurting others. Call it sin. This is where Jesus, the Son of God, comes in. He came willingly, primarily to pay the debt for my sins and yours, giving us the opportunity to repent and believe, to say, "Sorry, Lord; please forgive me," and to invite Jesus Christ into our hearts and lives so He by the Spirit can live in us and through us.

This process gives you and me new hearts, hearts that learn to love the light and hate the darkness. Therefore your outstanding debt and mine to the perfect One is not paid by you and me, but by the Son of God, who loves us and willingly died for us.

Once you say yes to Jesus and invite Him to be Lord and Savior of your life, He will come in. This becomes the doorway of access to the multiple and bountiful blessings of God that are promised in the Bible to every believer. The process of becoming Christlike has begun.

At a conference in England in 1947 shortly before he died, Smith Wigglesworth, a famous British evangelist, gave a prophetic word about unprecedented revival sweeping the UK, Europe, and the world. It would be like nothing we have ever seen before. "When the Word and the Spirit come together, there will be the biggest movement of the Holy Spirit that the nation, and indeed the world, has ever seen."[1] (Look it up and read the entire word.)

It is now seventy years since Wigglesworth gave that word. Something massive and transformational is about to break open and sweep the earth, and it will not be a compromised, watered-down, powerless, popular "Gospel" that is non-offensive and politically correct. No, but an in-your-face, mighty outpouring of the Word and the Spirit that is full of truth, power, love, and miracles.

Come on, friends, now that you've picked up this copy of *Whatever Happened to the Gospel?*, read it! Be like the five wise virgins in Matthew 25 and buy this oil. Become full of the Word and the Spirit. Be on fire for God, anxiously awaiting the return of your Bridegroom. Buy this good news oil, get yourself back on track, and together let's win this world for Jesus!

By the way, the last chapter in the book is a fantastic chapter on Heaven. Don't miss it!

—JOHN ARNOTT
CATCH THE FIRE, PARTNERS IN HARVEST, TORONTO

PREFACE

THIS BOOK IS being published in recognition of an important date in church history—the five hundredth anniversary of the historic contribution of Martin Luther (1483–1546). He nailed his Ninety-Five Theses to the door of the Castle Church in Wittenberg, Germany, on October 31, 1517. It led to the Great Reformation of the sixteenth century, which turned the world upside down. Martin Luther is one of my heroes, and I can confidently state that what I write in this book honors his rediscovery of the Gospel of Jesus Christ.

But why call this book *Whatever Happened to the Gospel?* Ever since I raised the question "Whatever happened to the Gospel?" at my farewell service at Westminster Chapel in January 2002, I have been yearning to turn this phrase into a book. As the saying goes, "The main thing is to keep the main thing the main thing." If the reason *God sent His Son into the world to die on a cross, that we might believe in Him and not perish but have eternal life* (John 3:16), is not the main thing, I do not know what is. If being ready to die and face God at the final judgment (Heb. 9:27) is not the main thing, I don't know what is. I'm sorry, but the Gospel does not seem to be the main thing in many churches, with many church leaders, and for many Christians these days.

Satan has been at work overtime for some two thousand years to pervert, distort, or replace the historic Gospel of Jesus Christ with a different emphasis in the church than preaching the Gospel. This is to say nothing about the widespread emergence of a different gospel (Gal. 1:6) or a different Jesus (2 Cor. 11:4) all over the world. The more I travel, the more I read, the more I listen, and the more I watch religious television, the more my spirit is stirred within me. Jeremiah spoke of "fire shut up" in his bones (Jer. 20:9). That is the way I feel. I suppose every author believes that his or her latest book is the most important, but I cannot imagine a book more important than this one.

I have done my best to make this a positive book from start to finish. That said, I am compelled to warn of the present danger we face in the church today as clearly and tenderly as I can. So many in the church don't know their Bibles and are gullible and swept to and fro by every wind of doctrine. Do please bear with me when you come across sensitive spots, and prayerfully consider the validity of what I say in this book.

I want to thank Charisma House for publishing this book. As most readers will know, this esteemed publishing house is best known for championing works by charismatic writers. I am extremely blessed to be on this list because I am one of them. But I am also equally Reformed in my theology. Furthermore, one must never forget that Charisma House is Protestant and evangelical. It joins the ranks of many Christian writers who commemorated the five hundredth anniversary of Martin Luther's historic Ninety-Five Theses. As it happens, October 31 is my own anniversary for being baptized with the Holy Spirit, as I will share in this book.

Those who have followed my ministry over the years will know that I am a "Word and Spirit" man. I believe that the Word and Spirit must come together if we expect to see the honor of God's name restored to the church and in the world. People sometimes ask me, "What do you mean by *Word*?" My answer is the whole of Scripture generally and the Gospel of Jesus Christ particularly. This book is an example of what I mean by *the Word*.

A host of friends have given me wise input and criticism of the manuscript of this book. My former editor, Barbara Dycus, kindly came out of retirement to help me with this important book. Her encouragement and suggestions have been incalculably helpful. I thank Debbie Marrie also for her wonderful assistance in bringing this book to completion. Steve and Joy Strang of Charisma House are great friends, and I do thank them most warmly for publishing this book. My greatest gratitude is as always to my wife, Louise, my best friend and critic.

—R. T. KENDALL
OCTOBER 31, 2017

INTRODUCTION

"I EXPECT THREE SURPRISES when I get to Heaven." So Martin Luther, the German Reformer who turned the world upside down in the sixteenth century by his rediscovery of justification by faith alone, is often quoted as saying. First, there will be people in Heaven he did not expect to be there. Second, there will be people not present in Heaven he was certain would be there. Third is the greatest surprise of all—that he is there himself!

I write this book to show:

1. What the New Testament means by *the Gospel*

2. How you can be sure you will go to Heaven when you die

DEFINITION OF THE TRUE GOSPEL

The Gospel is the good news that you will go to Heaven when you die—and not to Hell—by transferring your trust in your good works to what Jesus Christ the Son of God did for you on the cross.

I want to commend most heartily and warmly those people in various parts of the world—especially in Britain and America, where I have many friends—who faithfully uphold and preach the historic Gospel of Jesus Christ. This would include those in the public ministry but equally those laypeople who have little or no profile in the church. I thank God for anyone and everyone who is unashamed of the pure Gospel of Jesus Christ—whether in pulpits preaching to thousands or giving out pamphlets in the streets.

If you are like me, you will be surprised to learn that the question "Whatever happened to the Gospel?" became relevant before the end of the first century of Christianity—even while the apostle John was still alive. However, it is sad but true that few were asking that question then. The Gospel was brushed to one side, and no one seemed to notice it. Proof of this is Jesus's letter to the church of Ephesus from the throne of God (Rev. 2:1–7), written sometime between AD 70 and AD 100.

Two thousand years later the question becomes more relevant than ever, especially when you watch some religious programs on TV today. I would say that at least 90 percent of what we watch on religious television focuses on almost everything but the Gospel. For example:

- The "prosperity gospel"
- The "health and wealth gospel"
- The "name it and claim it gospel"
- Hyper-grace teaching

- The "political gospel"
- The "feel-good gospel"

I'm sorry, but the common denominator of religious television today is mostly about money. Whatever happened to the Gospel? The Gospel is free!

The "prosperity gospel"—which suggests God will make you prosperous if you support a particular ministry—has eclipsed the Gospel of Jesus Christ on many religious television networks. The emphasis on worship and singing has done virtually the same thing in many churches when you consider how little time is given to preaching in some places—not to mention the shallow content of so many songs being written today. Hyper-grace teaching—the notion that believers do not need to confess their sins to God—has elbowed its way into many churches. It has divided the people of God in many parts of the world and in some cases even ruined marriages. The "political gospel," whether it is called that or not, relegates the Gospel to one side in order to stress how crucial it is that you vote for a particular party or candidate. The theology of "open theism" (defined later) has been the doctrinal foundation of many platforms, even if some don't know what this term means.

Furthermore, many people in Charismatic churches flock to hear a *rhema* word—a word of knowledge or personal prophecy—but sometimes show no interest in the real reason God sent His Son to die on the cross. "Name it and claim it" teaching suggests you can have anything you ask for; just name what you want and claim that God will give it to you. The "health and wealth gospel" purports that God wants everybody to be well off financially and healed. If one is not healed, it is due to one's lack of faith. Really?

In addition to these concerns, have you ever thought about the absence of preaching and teaching on Hell and eternal punishment? Have you become concerned about the lack of the fear of God in church and society? Have you wondered if there might be a correlation between the absence of the fear of God and the absence of belief in eternal punishment?

If this were not enough to concern us, there has been an ever-growing acceptance of universalism in the church today—the view that all will be saved and none will be lost. This teaching renders the Gospel useless! Why preach if all will be saved?

And yet I have also been worried about a large number of "Word" churches, also "Spirit" churches, especially in America, that have been more excited about politics than the Gospel. There are those who feel they have a mandate to support certain candidates owing to their conservative views. I wish they were as excited about the Gospel as they are about who gets elected to political office. Right or left, rightly or wrongly, it seems to me that the Gospel has been pushed behind the door in order for people to express their political views. It somehow does not seem right to me to be more excited about political and social issues than the pure, simple, undiluted Gospel of Jesus Christ.

The true Gospel has been largely ignored in many historic Protestant churches in America and Great Britain—Methodists, Baptists, Presbyterians, Episcopals—some taking out any reference to the blood of Christ from the traditional hymns. At the same time, the focus in some Word churches has stressed sanctification as the only grounds for assurance of salvation, robbing the Gospel of its uniqueness. That said, it is my own observation that almost anywhere I go nowadays, a shocking percentage of people in all denominations—whether Word or Spirit churches—lack assurance of their own salvation simply because they don't know the Gospel.

Thankfully there are still a number of preachers, teachers, and lay Christians who have not allowed themselves to be diverted from the true Gospel. They believe now—and always have—in the true Gospel as defined at the start of this chapter. It is my sincere hope that this book will be a wake-up call for many others to be sure that the main thing—the true Gospel—once again becomes the real thing to them.

Several years ago I was invited by the late John Wimber to have dinner with him in London. I had heard him preach in the Royal Albert Hall and enjoyed his message. To be candid, I don't often get "words" for people. But I was pretty sure I had a word for John. I was troubled about one thing—and told him this: "You say, John, that 'the Reformers gave us the *Word* in the sixteenth century, but in the twentieth century we are to do the *works.*'" John agreed that this is what he had said and that his ministry was to teach people to do the *works*—largely praying for people to be healed. I said to him: "You are teaching pharaohs that knew not Joseph." (See Exod. 1:8.) "You are assuming that the people you are teaching *know the Word.* John, these people you are teaching don't have a clue what Martin Luther gave to the world in the sixteenth century.

How can you teach people to do the works when they don't actually know the Word?"

He put his knife and fork down, then put both of his index fingers in the middle of his chest and said to me: "RT, you have touched the very vortex of my thinking right now. I fully accept your word." Whether this made any difference in his ministry after that I do not know. I will say we became good friends. He spent two hours with me at Westminster Chapel a few weeks before he went to Heaven.

The Gospel as I defined it and will continue to mention in this book has, I believe, passed behind a cloud throughout the world. I refer to the historic Gospel as introduced by Jesus, filled out by the apostle Paul in the New Testament, and articulated by the Reformers of the sixteenth century.

My understanding of the Gospel has been refined over the past sixty years or more. As we will see, John Calvin (1509–1564) built his understanding of the Gospel on Martin Luther's teaching of justification by faith alone, not contradicting but making clearer what the apostle Paul and Luther taught.

I suspect Luther was right in his speculation. I think many of us may be surprised to see people in Heaven we assumed were not fit for Heaven. Could this be because *we* set a standard of fitness that is different from what the Lord Himself requires?

And yet if we should miss seeing a friend or loved one, I can only conclude that we will be kept from feeling any pain. God promised that He will wipe away all tears in the New Jerusalem and that there will be no pain (Rev. 21:4). I don't think God would let that question enter our minds in Heaven.

Paul's statement is worth remembering as you read this book:

> Therefore do not pronounce judgment before the time, before the Lord comes, who will bring to light the things now hidden in darkness and will disclose the purposes of the heart. Then each one will receive his commendation from God.
> —1 CORINTHIANS 4:5

CHAPTER ONE

REDISCOVERING THE TRUE GOSPEL

*I am astonished that you are so quickly deserting
him who called you in the grace of Christ and
are turning to a different gospel—not that there
is another one, but there are some who trouble
you and want to distort the gospel of Christ.*
—GALATIANS 1:6–7

A DRUNKEN MAN WANDERED around in a German village at two o'clock in the morning. He made his way to the parish church and walked in. He began climbing the stairs that led to the top of the belfry. He suddenly tripped. He grabbed a rope as he fell. It was the rope that rang the bell. Trying to save his life, he held on to the rope, which began going up and down as the bell began to ring. Lights went on throughout the village. A bell ringing in the middle of the night meant that something significant was happening. The whole village was awakened. People made their way to the church—only to find the drunken man holding on to the bell to save his life.

MARTIN LUTHER

Martin Luther's rediscovery of the apostle Paul's teaching of justification by faith alone woke up not only Germany but the whole of Europe. But Martin Luther did not intend to wake up the world; he was trying to save his own soul. That is all it was.

The son of a coal miner, Luther was born November 10, 1483, in Eisleben, Saxony, Germany.[1] To please his father, he entered law school at the University of Erfurt. But he eventually dropped out, complaining that law represented uncertainty. He sought assurance about life and was drawn to theology and philosophy. His tutors taught him to be suspicious even of the greatest thinkers and to test everything by experience. He became disillusioned with philosophy; it taught him nothing about loving God, which had become very important to him. He became convinced that he could know God only by revelation and reading the Holy Scriptures.[2]

At the age of twenty-one, on July 2, 1505, Luther was riding on horseback during a thunderstorm. Lightning struck very close to him. Being terrified of death and divine judgment, he cried out, "Help me, St. Anne, and I will become a monk!"[3] St. Anne was the patron saint of coal miners. He explained to his father that it was a vow he must keep. Two weeks later—on July 17—he became an Augustinian monk.[4] He devoted himself to fasting, long hours of prayer, and confession.[5] He was so conscientious that he would return to confession an hour after having just confessed to a priest, having thought of a sin he did not confess. The priests who heard his confession dreaded seeing him coming so often, and they sometimes tried to get out of having to hear Luther again.[6] In 1507 Luther was ordained to the priesthood. In 1508 he was invited to teach theology at the University of Wittenberg. On October 19, 1512, he was awarded a doctorate of theology.[7]

Luther became increasingly troubled about the spiritual condition of the church. He wondered about the rightness and biblical soundness of the sale of indulgences—paying for remission of temporal punishment due to sin, the money going to build St. Peter's in Rome.[8] It was suggested that he himself visit Rome. His colleagues felt he needed a break from his studies and that seeing the grandeur of Rome would encourage him. He went there.[9] While there he climbed the Scala Sancta, the "holy stairs."[10] (I myself did this when I was in Rome a few years ago. I wondered what it would seem like, especially recalling what Luther said to himself when he reached the top of the stairs.) These stairs had been built so that one could climb each step on his knees. It takes several minutes to do this on your knees. Each step allegedly guaranteed so many years out of purgatory.[11] When Luther reached the top of the stairs, he asked himself, "Who knows whether this be true?"[12] He also became disillusioned when he learned about the immorality of so many priests there. Being in Rome did not change his concerns but only heightened them.[13] He later reported, "I went to Rome smelling of onions; I came back smelling of garlic."[14]

LUTHER'S "TOWER EXPERIENCE"

At some point between 1513 and 1517, when he especially studied the Psalms, Romans, and Galatians, Luther had what he would call a "tower experience." No one seems to know the exact date. But we know it was while studying certain psalms—especially Psalm 32 and Psalm 118—and Romans and Galatians that he crossed over from doubt to full assurance of faith.[15] As for Psalm 118, "I call it my own," he said.[16] He became drawn particularly to Romans 1:17 (KJV): "The just shall live by faith," a quotation from Habakkuk 2:4, which is quoted three times in the New Testament: in Romans 1:17, Galatians 3:11, and Hebrews 10:38. His tower experience came when he became convinced that faith alone, apart from good works, satisfied the "passive justice of God."[17] By this Luther means that *he did not have to act* to satisfy God's justice; God is satisfied not by our having to perform works, but faith alone satisfied God's justice. *Active justice* would have meant what one *does* in order to get satisfaction. *Passive justice* would be getting satisfaction by doing nothing; it is when God sees our faith. "It is a passive justice by which the merciful God justifies us by faith,"[18] Luther concluded. Faith without works therefore means justification by *sola fidei*—"faith alone." When he began to perceive the implications of this insight, he became bolder and more confident.

His breakthrough therefore came by understanding Romans 1:17 (KJV): "The just shall live by faith"—that is, faith *alone*. That one word, *alone*, did it for Luther. Once he saw the implications of this, he never looked back. He was never the same again, nor would the Western

World—starting very soon after his own breakthrough—ever be the same again.

THE DAY OF DAYS

On October 31, 1517, at the age of thirty-three, Luther posted his famous Ninety-Five Theses on the door—some say it was more like a notice board—of the Wittenberg Castle Church.[19] He did not have any idea what was about to happen when he did this. Written in Latin only for scholars,[20] it was a list of questions and statements about people purchasing indulgences as a way of having their temporal sins forgiven and shortening their time in purgatory. At the bottom of these theses, summed up, was, "If the pope has power over purgatory, why ever doesn't he simply let everybody out?"[21] Luther's motive in writing the Ninety-Five Theses was to get a debate going about indulgences. But someone translated these into German, then printed them and distributed them without his permission. The knowledge of this little treatise spread like wildfire. In three weeks this was read all over Germany.[22] The ordinary, common people in particular were amazed and excited. This caused a stir among the highest levels of the church.[23] In two months it was read by the pope. It was the beginning of an awakening that eventually turned the Western World upside down. And yet it began with Martin Luther merely trying to save his own soul.

The Gospel and issue of personal salvation came to the forefront. Whereas the Eucharist (the Lord's Supper) had been the center of worship in churches, preaching became popular, preaching that explained the Bible. This, in turn, brought about an emphasis on ordinary people reading the Scriptures.[24] Previously people thought that only the priests could read the Bible and understand it. Luther later translated the entire Bible into German. Ordinary people began reading the Bible and, with the help of preaching, began to understand it![25] What became the Great Reformation was begun with the common people of Germany.

Although it was Martin Luther's breakthrough with Romans 1:17 that was so life changing, Paul's letter to the Galatians was Luther's favorite book.[26] Whereas Romans contains the "purest gospel," Galatians "is my Katie von Bora," he would say.[27] He married her in 1525.[28] He lectured through Galatians three times, dealing a lot with the issue of the Mosaic Law and the Gospel. Here are three interesting quotes of Luther on this subject:

> Whoever knows how to distinguish skillfully between the Law and the Gospel, by the grace of God he also knows how to be a theologian.

> Anybody who wishes to be a theologian...must distinguish between the Law and the Gospel.

> There's no man living on earth who knows how to distinguish between the Law and the Gospel.

It is hard to read the third quote without laughing! But Luther was beautifully transparent in all he wrote and did. After he was excommunicated from the Catholic Church in 1521,[29] he said, "Katie and I are going to get married. We are going to have babies. We will put the nappies in our front garden for the pope to see!"

It was at the Diet (official meeting of the Holy Roman emperor) of Worms, Germany, from April 16–18, 1521, that things came to a head.[30] Luther stood before the authorities. On a table nearby were twenty-five of his tracts, including the Ninety-Five Theses, *On the Papacy of Rome, The Babylonian Captivity of the Church*, and *On the Freedom of a Christian*. "Dr. Luther, will you denounce what you have written in these tracts?"[31]

He asked for twenty-four hours to think about it. During those twenty-four hours he prayed and felt little or no sense of the presence of God. He wrote out his prayer. He cried out in his cell; among other things he said, "My God, art Thou dead? No, You cannot die; You only hide yourself."[32]

The meeting recommenced the next day, on April 18, 1521. He was asked to deny what he had written in the tracts. His reply was something like this:

> Unless I am convinced by the testimony of the Scriptures or by clear reason (for I do not trust either in the pope or in councils alone, since it is well known that they have often erred and contradicted themselves), I am bound by the Scriptures I have quoted and my conscience is captive to the Word of God. I cannot and I will not recant anything, since it is neither safe nor right to go against conscience. [Here I stand. I can do no other.] May God help me. Amen.[33]

After this Luther was kidnapped by friends (to keep him from being executed) and was hidden in Wartburg Castle.[34] During the next eleven months he translated the

Bible into German.[35] Germany and all of Europe were never to be the same again.

The Gospel of Jesus Christ became the paramount issue. It set him free.

My book is not only a commemoration of Luther's faith and courage; I equally believe that it is an extension of what he began in the sixteenth century. We need a new Reformation today. The battle lines are not the same in every generation. Luther also said, "Where the battle rages, there the loyalty of the soldier is proved."[36]

Never forget: it was Luther finding rest of his soul that started the entire movement. He needed to know that he was accepted before God more than he wanted anything else in the world.

Some Important Questions

I ask, Have you ever been concerned about your own soul and final destiny? Jesus asked an unanswerable question: "For what does it profit a man to gain the whole world and forfeit his soul?" (Mark 8:36). "It is appointed for man to die once, and after that comes judgment" (Heb. 9:27). "We will all stand before the judgment seat of God" (Rom. 14:10).

I therefore ask you this question: If you were to stand before God—and you will—and He were to ask you (He could), "Why should I let you into My Heaven?" what would you say? There is only one valid answer.

What is your answer to this question?

This book, at bottom, deals with two questions:

1. What makes a person fit for Heaven?

2. What happens to those who do not go to Heaven?

MY THEOLOGICAL BACKGROUND

My own background—for which I still thank God with all my heart—helps qualify me to write this book, this being something I feel I should share.

I became a Christian on Easter Sunday, April 5, 1942, at the age of six. Before going to church that day, I, in tears, said to my parents, "I want to be a Christian." My father said, "We don't need to wait until we get to church; you can do this now." I knelt with my parents at their bedside and confessed my sins. As I look back, I can't imagine there were many sins I was conscious of—only talking back to my parents and feeling ashamed. I was convicted of this. I wept as I prayed. I felt a sense of peace and relief. I never looked back. I believe I was truly converted that day. But how much of the Gospel I knew at the time is another question.

I was brought up in the Church of the Nazarene. I was named after my father's favorite preacher, R. T. Williams, general superintendent of the Church of the Nazarene. I have always cherished my Nazarene background. In fact, it is what largely endeared me to Dr. Martyn Lloyd-Jones (1899–1981). He had read a biography of Phineas Bresee (1838–1915), the founder of the Church of the Nazarene. Dr. Lloyd-Jones felt that there was something genuine about Bresee and the early Nazarenes, that there was a real touch of God on them. Dr. Lloyd-Jones used to say to me again and again, "Don't forget your Nazarene background. It is what has saved you," meaning that it saved me from being like too many Reformed pastors who he thought were "perfectly orthodox, perfectly useless."

I entered Trevecca Nazarene College (now University) in Nashville, Tennessee, in September 1953. A year and a half later, in March 1955, while remaining a student at Trevecca, I was called to be the pastor of the Church of the Nazarene in Palmer, Tennessee, about 115 miles from Nashville. I drove to Palmer on weekends while attending classes at Trevecca from Monday through Friday.

On a Monday morning, October 31, 1955, while driving in my car back to Nashville, I had what I would describe as a Damascus Road experience, although it was not my conversion. It was my baptism with the Holy Spirit, what Dr. Lloyd-Jones would call "the sealing of the Holy Spirit." On old US 41, a few miles from the bottom of Monteagle, Tennessee, the Lord Jesus appeared to me as I drove. I saw Him interceding for me at the right hand of God. An hour later I entered into a rest of faith; my heart was warmed, and peace came into my heart unlike anything I had ever experienced. Before sundown that same day, my theology changed. I knew I was eternally saved, and I was given a glimpse of the sovereignty of God. For days I wondered if I had discovered something new, if I might be the first since the apostle Paul to believe these things!

Because of the views I was discovering for myself, my Trevecca professor William M. Greathouse cautioned me, "RT, you are going off into Calvinism." I had never read anything by John Calvin or a book by any Calvinist. I knew that the Pilgrims who came to America on the

Mayflower were known as Puritans, but I had not read a book by any Puritan. Months later I was to learn I had not discovered anything new at all but that I was led to the mainstream of Protestant theology. It is still an amazing feeling to this day when I try to absorb having seen these truths without reading books.

My own theological background, without doubt, helped prepare me for the writing of this book. I was brought up in a church that taught that one gets to Heaven by being "saved" and "sanctified wholly"—these being two works of grace. The second work of grace was also called "second-blessing holiness," without which no one shall see the Lord (Heb. 12:14). The second work of grace allegedly enabled one to "live above sin." If one did sin, the person lost his or her salvation, and he or she was now headed for Hell. Some taught that the sin nature was "eradicated" by the second work of grace,[37] although surprisingly this did not keep a person from sinning.

One of the sad consequences of my old teaching was that the Gospel of Jesus Christ was—I'm sorry—barely mentioned. It was almost entirely about holy living instead—not going to the cinema, and the women not wearing makeup. These are some of my most indelible memories. I choose to believe that the Gospel was preached now and then. The need to be saved was certainly emphasized, or I would not have told my parents on that Easter Sunday that I wanted to be a Christian. I have asked myself many times whether I ever heard the true Gospel preached by the four different pastors I heard as I grew up in Ashland, Kentucky. Surely I did. But I am simply not sure.

The question follows: How could one ever become a

Christian in an atmosphere in which the pure Gospel is rarely, if ever, preached? Good question.

It is John Calvin's teaching of "implicit faith," to be explained later, that shows how a person could be regenerate without fully understanding the Gospel as the apostle Paul knew it. This explains how I could be saved at such a young age without hearing the true Gospel as I now understand it. How much could one know at the age of four, the age of Jonathan Edwards when he was first overwhelmed by the glory of the Lord?

Martin Luther had a lot more to learn—as we will see further later—especially regarding the Book of James. Calvin learned from Luther and made his teaching of justification by faith clearer than ever. Yet we are all learning. Each time we gain a fresh insight, our reaction often is, "Why didn't I see this before?" and "Was I truly converted before then?" But new insights are partly what is meant by being changed "from glory to glory" by the Spirit of the Lord (2 Cor. 3:18, KJV), or, as the ESV translates it, "from one degree of glory to another." It does not take a lot of knowledge to be saved. The least degree of faith in a great God is all that is required. Or, to extract two lines from the great hymn "Come, Ye Sinners, Poor and Needy":

> If you tarry till you're better,
> You will never come at all....
> All the fitness He requireth
> Is to feel your need of Him.
> —JOSEPH HART (1712–1768)[38]

CHAPTER TWO

MISUNDERSTANDING THE GOSPEL

Are we to continue in sin that grace may abound?
—ROMANS 6:1

WHEN MY LITTLE book, *Tithing*, first emerged from the press, I wanted a special friend in America to see the colorful cover and to show him that Billy Graham, John Stott, and Sir Fred Catherwood had endorsed my book.[1] I blush to admit this, but I was showing off, being so proud of this "coup," as my publisher put it. But my sending this to him backfired—hugely. Far from being impressed, he and his family interpreted my motive as scolding him for not tithing. The truth is that thought never crossed my mind. But my motive was still very wrong; I was only showing off. The funny thing was I did not get shot down for showing off but for what his family perceived. As they say nowadays, perception is reality. I was totally misunderstood. It certainly taught me a lesson.

The Gospel of Jesus Christ often gets misunderstood—hugely. It depends how it is presented. The Gospel is amazingly simple. Some might say too simple. Surely it is our works God wants! Or our money that God wants; that is certainly what many people thought in Germany in the sixteenth century. The church urged people to purchase indulgences.[2] They taught that God wants our good deeds as payment for salvation.[3] Or something that shows that what *we do*—not what He did—makes the difference.

Therefore the Gospel is frequently misunderstood. One of the main reasons it is misunderstood is because it seems too good to be true—that we are saved by another person's work. That someone *else* paid our debt. That someone purchased our home in Heaven by His own blood. Our natural instinct often tells us that there must be more to it than that. "Where's the catch?" we ask.

Yet if the Gospel you hear does not seem too good to be true, you probably have not heard it yet.

The purpose of this chapter is to demonstrate how the pure Gospel is often set to one side and forgotten in the course of history.

THE DEVIL HATES THE GOSPEL

I hope you, the reader, will bear with me as we look at some relevant historical events that show what I mean. The devil hates the pure Gospel of Christ. He will do whatever it takes to distort it, camouflage it, hide it, add to it, turn it into works, stigmatize it, divert you from it, or masquerade it, as when Satan appears as an angel of light (2 Cor. 11:14).

It is very, very hard to take this in: we are assured of going to Heaven simply by relying on Jesus's blood. Our natural instinct tells us there is more to it, that we must do something to earn it or to prove to ourselves that we are saved. This is called *self-righteousness.*

But at the other extreme comes the notion of some— of those who *do* understand the Gospel to a degree—that not only is holy living irrelevant, but so too is confessing our sins! Since Jesus died for all our sins, why confess them? That has become known in our day as "hyper-grace" teaching—a very dangerous heresy. It is pure anti-nomianism, as we will see later.

You can therefore see why this Gospel is often misunderstood.

The way this misunderstanding plays out is usu-ally giving in to one of two extremes: self-righteousness or blatant sinning. The hymn writer Augustus Toplady (1740–1778), famous for his hymn "Rock of Ages, Cleft for Me," noted these two extremes: Phariseeism and anti-nomianism, asserting:

> Christ is still crucified between two thieves.[4]

PHARISEEISM

Phariseeism is a teaching or practice that is like that of the ancient Pharisees. The Pharisees were among Jesus's chief enemies. They were seen as the most pious people of the day. No one doubted how outwardly righteous they were. But Jesus exposed this as being "like whitewashed tombs, which outwardly appear beautiful, but within are full of dead people's bones and all uncleanness" (Matt. 23:27–28). Jesus was onto them, and they knew it. They hated Him;

He hated not them but their self-righteousness. Everything they do, said Jesus, is done "to be seen by others" (Matt. 23:5). The Pharisees sincerely thought they were a cut above all others in their day because of their outward piety. They tithed. Fasted twice a week. Kept the Law to the hilt (so they thought). They believed that good works saved them.

Some readers may know of my book with Rabbi Sir David Rosen of Jerusalem, titled *The Christian and the Pharisee* (his idea for the title).[5] We exchanged letters to each other, which became a book. I sought to prove to him that Jesus is Israel's Messiah. He shows why he disagrees. He unashamedly sees himself as a Pharisee. The Pharisee in the New Testament "does not get a good press," he says to me. Yet Rabbi Rosen states explicitly that atonement, to him, is simply doing good works.

THE ENGLISH PURITANS

I came to Oxford in 1973 to study the English Puritans. For years they had been my heroes. But that was before I examined them very carefully. Studying these notable men—such as William Perkins (1558–1602), the most influential of the English Puritans; and Thomas Hooker (1586–1647), who became the founder of the state of Connecticut—led me to a measure of disillusionment. These men had in common the belief that a person must be "prepared" for grace before he or she could be truly saved.[6] Such preparation to me smacked of salvation by works.

I will never forget reading the sermons of Hooker one afternoon in the British Museum in London. After many days and hours of reading Hooker, trying to make sense of his teaching on preparation—and how one must attain to a certain level of godliness *before* one had a warrant to be saved, I became not only disillusioned but sickened. I remember it as though it were yesterday. I put my hands on the edge of the table, pushed my chair back, looked up at the ceiling, and asked myself, "Is this why I came to England? Is this what I am supposed to preach? I may as well have stayed in my old denomination." I packed my books and left for the day.

And yet I have to say that the teaching of preparation for grace is alive and well in some places today. Some teach that you cannot claim to be a Christian until you prove it by your perseverance. If you turn out well, good; this shows you were truly born again. But if you don't turn out well, this shows you were not truly saved after all. I do not accept this kind of teaching. That is precisely what I was set free from. It is certainly not "good news." If I am told I cannot be sure I am saved unless I am always manifesting holiness—good works—that is bondage. I would be looking inside myself day and night to see if I am still saved, checking my spiritual pulse every day, asking, "Am I in, or am I out?" What a terrible way to live! I know it well.

That is not what this book is about. The Gospel is the Good News that by transferring my trust in good works to what Jesus did on the cross, I *will* go to Heaven and not to Hell. I call that Good News. But when I am told I have to *add* good works to my faith in order to *know* I have true faith, the "good news" becomes heavy news. Sad news. No joy. No assurance. That is the way I was brought up; it is not what I believe today.

There is a widespread teaching today called "lordship salvation." Sadly those who teach this do not say it means affirming that Jesus is God, which (in my opinion) is what Paul actually means by *lordship salvation*. They say you cannot claim to have Jesus as your Savior until you first receive Him as Lord. Agreed. But what does it mean to acknowledge Him as Lord? Does it mean you must obey all His commands before you can be sure you are saved? There are those who virtually put sanctification before salvation as proof you are really saved!

A well-known story in Puritan folklore comes to mind. Hooker's father-in-law cautioned him that his teaching was very like that of Thomas Shepard (1605–1649). Shepard's teaching on preparation "made as good Christians before they come to Christ as ever they were after by his preaching," said Hooker's father-in-law.[7] I cannot help but wonder, then, if Thomas Shepard's order of salvation is not essentially the same emphasis as some of those who propound "lordship salvation." Therefore the previous insinuation referring to Shepard was that those whom these men would say did not have saving grace were possibly already Christians! At least their preparation changed their lives. But they never knew for sure when—if ever—they had assurance. Indeed, virtually all of the Puritans I read taught preparation for grace. The unsurprising result was that their hearers continually struggled to know whether they were saved. They feared they were of the non-elect—those not chosen by God to be saved—who had only the appearances of conversion but were still unsaved. The highly respected William Perkins, who was the fountain-head of this perspective, went to his grave not knowing whether he himself was saved. (Please see my *Calvin and English Calvinism to 1649* for details.[8]) In order to get assurance from "lordship salvation" teaching, such hope is to be inevitably traced to some degree of self-righteousness.

This is not the intent of the Gospel of Jesus Christ as taught in the New Testament generally and by the apostle Paul particularly. Paul said, "I am not ashamed, for I know whom I have believed and am persuaded that He is able to keep what I have committed to Him until that Day" (2 Tim. 1:12, NKJV).

ANTINOMIANISM

The notion that it does not matter whether you live a godly life since you are justified by faith alone (which is called *antinomianism* in theological circles) was bound to come up. It is no doubt true that the fear of antinomianism (literally "against law") is what caused Martin Luther's discovery in the sixteenth century to be eclipsed by legalism in the seventeenth century. Popularly understood, antinomianism is the notion that it does not matter how you live since you are justified by faith alone. The irony is those people in the sixteenth and seventeenth centuries who were accused of this were seen as godly people. But the theory of licentious living was often attached to the term. Ironically it was a term that Luther himself coined, emerging out of the fear that people would abuse the teaching of justification by faith alone and not live lives that reflect the standard set by the Ten Commandments.

Since we are saved by faith alone and not works, will not people give in to sin? No doubt, some have done so. Even Paul faced a similar charge in his day and condemned those who abused the Gospel in such a manner (Rom. 3:8).

However, Dr. Martyn Lloyd-Jones used to say that if our Gospel is not accused of being antinomian, chances are we have not preached it![9] But he went on to say that if you think that antinomianism is what Paul actually taught, you have misunderstood him!

The fear of antinomianism has had a considerable effect—all over Europe and England in the sixteenth century and all over the world to the present day. It is a valid fear. But some have been so afraid of being accused of antinomianism that they end up with a gospel of works and not grace. And the Gospel ceases to be Good News.

The consequence of the fear of antinomianism in the seventeenth century was that Luther's bold teaching was swept under the carpet. The Gospel seemed too good to be true, and legalism set in. Although what Luther taught was generally upheld theoretically by Protestants, it was nonetheless brushed to one side by stressing that one must manifest holy living to have a *warrant for assurance* of salvation. The result was that people feared they were never holy enough to be sure they were saved. However, some also taught that you could be a "reprobate"—a term Puritans used to refer to the non-elect—and *still* manifest the fruits of sanctification. This is why people who followed this line of thought almost always lacked assurance. They were terrified that they could be predestined to damnation even though they were living holy lives. So what Luther taught—that we are justified by faith alone—was generally adhered to, but the question was now asked, "How do *you* know you have *true faith*?" The nature of faith became the issue. To Luther the issue was the nature of justification. The question pertaining to the nature of true faith—*How do you know you have it?*—sadly trumped Luther's rediscovery of Paul's teaching. The melancholy result was that the freedom that Luther gave to the church became a new kind of bondage.

THE APOSTOLIC FATHERS

The term *apostolic fathers* refers to leading figures in the early church who were converted either by one of the Twelve, e.g. John, or by someone who was very close to that period. "Whatever happened to the Gospel?" is a question that should have been asked before AD 100. It would seem that the Gospel that Paul taught began to disappear before the first century of the church passed. Paul had warned about a falling away, or rebellion (2 Thess. 2:3). I will not enter into the discussion whether such a falling away is eschatological (pertaining to the very last days) or whether its fulfillment in some sense came at the end of the first century. But one thing is certain: to understand the Gospel—because it seems too good to be true—and to maintain such a Gospel is something that one must guard with jealous care. It is so easy to add to the Gospel because the pure, undiluted Gospel seems too good to be true.

Paul's chief enemies were people called Judaizers. That is the name we give them today. They were Jews who claimed to be Christians. Whether they were truly converted is debatable. They tried to turn Gentile Christians into Jews by requiring that they be circumcised. They accused Paul of not teaching the Law. Far from believing in justification by faith alone, they required that Gentiles *submit to the Mosaic Law first* if they hoped to be saved. They were a thorn in Paul's side; some think he had them in mind when he referred to his thorn in the flesh in 2 Corinthians 12:7. These troublemakers only fished in the Christian pond. Seeing people saved did not come to their minds. They followed Paul around and infiltrated his converts. These men, then, were professing Jewish Christians who insisted you must bring in the Mosaic Law, or it was false teaching. Paul confronted it all the time, but it is perhaps most obvious in his letter to the Galatians. It was these Judaizers that Paul had in mind when he warned of "a different gospel" intruding (Gal. 1:6).

I don't know that we have the exact equivalent of Judaizers today. The now-defunct Worldwide Church of God came pretty close. Yet I worry about any group that wants to bring the ancient holy days into our worship, such as people who want to observe the Jewish Sabbaths, Jewish feasts, or whatever was regarded as a holy day in ancient Israel. These have been nailed to the cross (Col. 2:14).

I will say it again: the devil hates the Gospel. The flesh would never invent such a Gospel. Many years after His ascension to Heaven, Jesus addressed seven churches in Asia. He said to the church of Ephesus, "You have abandoned the love you had at first. Remember therefore from where you have fallen" (Rev. 2:4–5). As I said, this admonishment may have been as early as AD 70 but no later than AD 100. When you consider the Gospel in the Book of Ephesians and the time Paul took with this church (see

Acts chapters 19 and 20), it is rather surprising that Jesus would need to rebuke them so soon as He did from His throne in Heaven.

I used to think that the closer we can get to the earliest church, the more likely we are to find those who best knew the Lord and therefore upheld the soundest theology. I have come to realize that is not necessarily the case. But because some of those whom I greatly admired—such as Ignatius of Antioch (d. 108) or Polycarp (d. 155)—were glorious martyrs of the faith, I assumed they would be the best possible examples of sound Christian doctrine following the first generation of the earliest church. It has been a lesson for me that those who die for Jesus Christ are not always theologically resourceful. Not that these men were not sound; I am merely saying that their writings did not sound much like Paul.

Professor Thomas F. Torrance (1913–2007) produced an epoch-making study of the early church in the second century, detailing the doctrines of grace in the apostolic fathers.[10] The apostolic fathers include not only the godly martyrs I just mentioned but other major figures of the second century—such as Clement of Rome (d. 100) and Shepherd of Hermas (first late century or mid–second century). There was also the *Didache*, known as "the teaching of the Twelve" (possibly first century). All these are valuable sources for the understanding of the earliest church following the apostolic era. But do you find the teaching of the apostle Paul in the writings of these men? It is almost like looking for a needle in a haystack. The conclusion of Professor Torrance as to the doctrines of grace in the apostolic fathers: there was virtually none.[11]

The era of the apostolic fathers also included some of the worst kinds of heretics, such as Marcion (c. 85–c. 160). He was an enemy of the Gospel and caused havoc in the early church. But the German church historian Adolf von Harnack (1851–1930) made the arresting observation that the ancient heretic Marcion, although known for his bizarre teachings, was the first post-apostolic figure to understand the apostle Paul! "And yet it must be said that he misunderstood him," continues Harnack. This is what we must never forget about antinomianism. To repeat Dr. Lloyd-Jones's observation: If the thought of antinomianism does not come to mind when you hear the Gospel, you have probably not heard the Gospel, but if you think that Paul taught antinomianism, you have still misunderstood it!

It is not until you get to the writings of St. Augustine of Hippo (354–430) that you find a man who began to understand Paul's doctrine of salvation. He also upheld Jesus's teaching on eternal punishment. Augustine faithfully upheld the gospel of grace. Not that Augustine was perfect or that you can take seriously all he wrote; he was nonetheless the first major figure in the Christian church to restore much of the pure Gospel of Jesus Christ to the church. For this reason men such as Martin Luther and John Calvin would quote St. Augustine all the time in order to show that they were not propagating something new. If they could prove that St. Augustine said it first, it made it easier for people to believe.

I have determined with all my heart to keep this book positive. Yet I must say that I have been very worried indeed that some popular preachers and respected scholars have reinterpreted Jesus and Paul in a manner that, if taken seriously by many, could eventually cause the true Gospel to disappear almost completely. A well-known and respected British New Testament scholar, arguably the greatest in the world today, has overthrown his Reformed background by his reinterpreting Paul. I'm afraid he has influenced a lot of sincere people, especially pastors. He completely overthrows Luther and denies justification by faith only. I know him fairly well—he and I were at Oxford together doing our research degrees at the same time. He asked to be introduced to Dr. Martyn Lloyd-Jones when the doctor was visiting me at our home in Headington, Oxford. A brilliant scholar, he was then in the embryonic phase of his innovative understanding of Paul. Dr. Lloyd-Jones was immediately worried about him, very concerned that this promising young man was reading more into Paul than Paul himself saw. "He is more clever than Paul," Dr. Lloyd-Jones said to me afterward. Yet I can tell you that it was the fear of antinomianism that partly drove him to his controversial position.[12]

I am therefore equally thinking of the church of tomorrow—should Jesus tarry—when I write this book.

CHAPTER THREE

RECOGNIZING AND AVOIDING THE COUNTERFEIT

For the time is coming when people will not endure sound teaching, but having itching ears they will accumulate for themselves teachers to suit their own passions.
—2 TIMOTHY 4:3

WHEN WE FIRST retired from Westminster Chapel, Louise and I lived in the Florida Keys. We had the most wonderful neighbors in Key Largo. I never succeeded in getting them to go to church unless I was preaching. They came to hear me out of courtesy. They insisted that they found a preacher on TV who fulfilled their spiritual needs. "We can't smoke if we go to church, but we can stay home and smoke and drink our gin and tonics while we listen to him." What is more, "he makes us feel *so good*." They referred to a popular preacher who begins weekly with the words that ostensibly affirm the Bible. Those words attract a lot of sincere people who are disillusioned with the church and want to follow someone who seems to believe the Bible. Thousands are taken in by them—and therefore feel safe. I will admit that I enjoy listening to him too. He is a terrific and winsome communicator. But after a while I cannot help but ask one question: Whatever happened to the Gospel? If only he would preach it!

There are at least two ominous trends in various places in recent years that you need to be aware of. One is a revival of an ancient idea first argued for by the second-century heretic Marcion, to whom I referred earlier. He was not only the first notable person in church history to reject certain books of the New Testament he didn't like but the first also to separate the New Testament from the Old Testament. He did not like the God of the Old Testament. The way this is carried out today is by separating Jesus from the Old Testament. The God of the Old Testament has been under a vicious attack for a long time. One can sense the increasing number of people who say, "Jesus, yes" but a resounding "No" to the God described in the Old Testament. I ask, Why did Jesus never apologize for the God of the Old Testament?

The answer is the God of the Old Testament was *His Father*, and He affirmed the Old Testament to the hilt.

There is another trend not dissimilar to the first, namely, the sweeping assertion "Jesus, yes" but "Paul, no." They love Jesus's teachings. They love Jesus the healer, the Jesus who accepted children, the Jesus who taught we should love our enemies, even the Jesus who bravely went to the cross. But many of these people disdain Paul's teachings. What they hate most is Paul's doctrine of the atonement, his doctrine of justification by faith, and his view of the sovereignty of God. This is nothing new. For over a century some scholars have made the claim that the Christian faith was doing very well until Saul of Tarsus was converted. When Saul became the apostle Paul, he messed everything up. As I show in my book *The Sermon on the Mount*, the only sure way to understand Jesus's teachings is through Paul's interpretation of the Mosaic Law.[1] Paul was as essential to the development of the Christian faith as the prophets were to the spiritual development of ancient Israel in the Old Testament.

Closely akin to the notion "Jesus, yes; Paul, no" are those who identify themselves as Red Letter Christians. What they mean in part is this: we take those statements of Jesus that are printed in red in some editions. As a matter of fact, I myself prefer those editions where Jesus's statements are in red print. But these Red Letter Christians go further than that. They appeal to Jesus's teachings to enforce their liberal and political views—those views, for example, that support homosexual marriages. They fancy that Jesus would be OK with certain liberal views, but not Paul. Not true. But my point is the Red Letter Christians are one more example of being selective with Scripture, as if we have a right to pick and choose which parts of the Word of God we will accept.

APOLOGIZE FOR THE GREAT REFORMATION?

Parallel with these threatening trends is the apparent need of some leaders today to apologize for the Great Reformation. Some say the church would have been better off without people such as John Wycliffe (1320–1384), Jan Hus (1369–1415), William Tyndale (1494–1536), Martin Luther,

Thomas Cranmer (1489–1556), John Knox (1513–1572), and John Calvin. I disagree. I thank God for these men. Indeed, God raised them up at a critical time in history. Wycliffe, known as the "morning star of the Reformation," translated the Bible from Latin Vulgate into English. Hus was burned at the stake partly for popularizing Wycliffe's views in Europe.[2] Tyndale translated the New Testament from the Greek into English and was burned at the stake for this and for endorsing the views of Martin Luther.[3] (One of our grandsons is named Tyndale.) Cranmer was burned at the stake in Oxford for his views of the Eucharist.[4] Knox was the founder of the Presbyterian Church in Scotland. Martin Luther's teaching of justification by faith changed the course of history in the sixteenth century— and Western civilization was all the better for it. John Calvin's elaboration on Luther's teaching gave England what was needed to establish the Gospel of Jesus Christ in that green and pleasant land.

When I think of Luther's expectation of being surprised when he gets to Heaven over who is there and who isn't, I wonder if I too will be surprised to see people in Heaven who sincerely thought their works saved them, or surprised not to see people there because they so consistently manifested good works. For example, I know that many of my old friends believe they will go to Heaven because they are "saved and sanctified." Should I be surprised to see them in Heaven? Furthermore, I think of countless people who have appeared to be solid Christians by their sacrifices and good deeds; should I be surprised if some of them are not in Heaven?

What, then, makes a person fit for Heaven? Caution:

> Therefore do not pronounce judgment before the time, before the Lord comes, who will bring to light the things now hidden in darkness and will disclose the purposes of the heart. Then each one will receive his commendation from God.
> —1 Corinthians 4:5

What about Luther's surmise that the biggest surprise of all is that he himself is there? Was he joking? Should he not know in advance that he will be there? If so, how could he be surprised? I answer—to quote Dr. Martyn Lloyd-Jones: A Christian is a person who is surprised that he is a Christian. Dr. Lloyd-Jones went so far as to question a person's salvation who is not surprised that he or she is a Christian! What is going on here? Is this a contradiction? I don't think so. A true Christian is continually surprised that he or she is a Christian—that is, amazed; he or she never gets over it. But at the same time the person knows in his or her heart what is gloriously true: the person is fit for Heaven because he or she has embraced the true Gospel.

The Centrality of Preaching

But whatever happened to the preaching of the Gospel? The Great Reformation resulted in a restoration of *preaching*. Satan is unhappy with any preaching of the Gospel. He will do whatever it takes whenever he can to keep the Gospel from being center stage. In the Middle Ages the Eucharist took the place of the Gospel. This is partly why the pulpits in the big cathedrals are not in the center but usually to the right or the left, with the central emphasis being on the Eucharist. The Great Reformation made the preaching of the Gospel central, and the architecture of many churches, especially in Switzerland, reflected this.

Yet as I said, the Reformation teaching of the sixteenth century, which set thousands of people free, especially through the teaching of justification by faith alone, went behind a cloud in the sixteenth century, especially in England. This was partly because Puritan teaching—which I call *experimental predestinarianism* in my book *Calvin and English Calvinism to 1649*—encouraged endless and unfulfilled introspection.[5] I repeat, whereas the teaching of salvation by true faith set people free, the Puritans raised the question "How do you know you have true faith?" And people were back to square one. The result was that virtually no one knew for sure that he or she had true faith. People were told to look for proofs of faith—loving God's Word; loving the Sabbath; showing "universal obedience," as in keeping *all* of the Ten Commandments; loving God's ministers; and turning away from every known sin. People were afraid they had not come up to the standard whereby one could say they had true faith by turning from every known sin. And the liberty that came with Reformation teaching turned into a new bondage.

WHATEVER HAPPENED TO THE GOSPEL?

If we fast-forward to the present day, the question "Whatever happened to the Gospel?" surfaces again—especially when you go to many churches or listen to much of Christian television. My friend Kenny Borthwick, a Church of Scotland minister, says he often watches Christian television as through the ears of an unbeliever. He concluded: "If

I did not know differently, based upon what I hear almost all of the time, I would conclude that Christianity is all about money."[6] I'm afraid this is true. So many TV ministers appeal to people's selfish interest, especially when it comes to finances, in order to get their prayer and financial support.

Therefore when I watch very much of Christian television, I ask, Whatever happened to the Gospel? I think much the same thing when I look carefully at the words of many popular religious songs that are written today. Some are so superficial and shallow. One of the latest is about Jesus loving us with a "sloppy, wet kiss."

Several years ago there were wide reports of "last-day ministries" being at hand, coming through preaching in Lakeland, Florida. We began to get phone calls, especially from people in England. God TV was telecasting the alleged "great revival" that had come in Lakeland. We began watching night after night. What was so amazing was this: never in my lifetime had I seen such an opportunity to reach the entire unevangelized world with the Gospel. Nations that never hear the Gospel were getting it in their homes. What an opportunity!

However, there was one thing missing: the preaching of the Gospel. The evangelist only had "words of knowledge" and prayers for healing. I waited and waited to hear the Gospel. How many times do you suppose I heard the Gospel? Only once, when a guest preacher took the place of the regular evangelist one evening. I asked myself, "If these are truly God's purposed 'last-day ministries,' surely God wants the Gospel of His Son preached, doesn't He?"

This is why I concluded—then and now—that the "revival" was not of God.

People cautioned me: "Don't say it's not of God; just say you are not sure." I stuck to my guns. It was not of God. There was *no conviction of sin, no preaching of the Gospel, and people were baptized in the name of the Father, Son, and BAM!*" (not the Holy Spirit but BAM). When the revival was abruptly shut down a few weeks later—owing to the immorality of the evangelist—people said to me, "RT, you were right."

But I asked, "Why did it take the evangelist's immorality to convince you? Couldn't you tell merely by listening to him?"

We are living in a generation that is almost entirely based upon "What's in it for me?"—probably the not surprising result of existential theology that has invaded the church. Existentialism centers on one's "existence"—being in the here and now. Not the future, not Heaven or Hell, not facing God at the Judgment, but *living in the here and now.* The "me generation" probably owes its existence to existential philosophy. The result is that people all over the world are swept to and fro by every wind of doctrine. I'm sorry, but I am astonished at the number of Christians I meet who do not know for sure what they believe. They cannot tell you. It is an epidemic of uncertainty in the church. What is sadder is whereas in the Middle Ages the common people did not have their own Bibles, in our generation everybody has a Bible but does not read it. It is common for ministers to take their "text" not from Scripture but another, more appealing source. Sermons are sometimes called "talks."

I can truly appreciate some of those people who espouse a "seeker-friendly" approach. After all, Paul said we should use all means to reach people (1 Cor. 9:22–23). Yes. But once we reach people and persuade them to hear us, is it the *true Gospel* they hear? That is the question.

CHAPTER FOUR

A FALSE TEACHING AT LARGE

And no wonder, for even Satan
disguises himself as an angel of light.
—2 CORINTHIANS 11:14

PICTURE THIS: An airplane takes off from John F. Kennedy International Airport in New York heading for London Heathrow. The navigator notices that the plane is just a minute degree off course after being in the air for a hundred miles. But this minute degree seems harmless. However, if the correction is not made immediately, six hours later the same plane will be flying over Spain rather than England.

That is how the original Gospel can eventually become unrecognizable, even though its proponents were only slightly off course in the beginning. Said Paul:

> For I feel a divine jealousy for you, since I betrothed you to one husband, to present you as a pure virgin to Christ. But I am afraid that as the serpent deceived Eve by his cunning, your thoughts will be led astray from a sincere and pure devotion to Christ. For if someone comes

and proclaims another Jesus than the one we pro-
claimed, or if you receive a different spirit from
the one you received, or if you accept a different
gospel from the one you accepted, you put up
with it readily enough.

—2 CORINTHIANS 11:2–4

Martin Luther managed to get back to the thinking of
Paul. But some of his followers went slightly off course in a
short period of time. It eventually becomes "another Jesus."

Yet some in the earliest church were way off course from
the beginning—as in the teaching of gnosticism, a heresy
that paralleled the Judaizers' distortion of the Gospel. They
were the first group of antinomians to have a high profile
in the first century. The Gnostics offered a "new way of
knowing." They said, "We can make the Christian faith
better." It almost destroyed the early church. They came
in through the back door, changing the grace of God into
lasciviousness (Jude 4). Parts of Colossians, some of 1 John,
and much of 2 Peter and Jude address the Gnostic danger.
These teachings were also condemned by the early fathers
in their own day. Yet some of these heresies have come
alive at the present time. One of the things we seem to
learn from church history is that we do not seem to learn
from church history.

In the earliest church there were also those only slightly
off course, such as some of the apostolic fathers. These
were good people, many dying at the stake for the Lord
Jesus Christ. But the slightest deviation from the apostles'
faith was more serious than they could have imagined.
The church was a long time in making needed corrections.

The false teaching I will discuss in this chapter is called hyper-grace teaching. I am *not* saying that those who teach these doctrines are not Christians. I am certainly not saying that those who follow them are not saved. But they are immature, being carried adrift by a wind of doctrine they don't seem to recognize as a departure from the pure Gospel of Jesus Christ. What I present next is a case of missing the mark by a huge degree, a serious case of not rightly dividing the word of truth (2 Tim. 2:15).

My prayer is that you will be able to grasp the truth of this book generally and the seriousness of error exposed in important parts of this book particularly.

Hyper-Grace Teaching

I'm not sure that the "hyper-grace" preachers want to be called that. Nor am I sure who gave it that name. I do not use the phrase to be offensive; I don't know what else to call it. Like it or not, the phrase will probably stick— that is, until this horrible teaching destroys itself. It is a teaching that has been very popular in the Far East— notably Singapore and Hong Kong. But it has spread to South Africa and America. Some Christian television networks are encouraging this teaching. It is only a matter of time until television producers will rue the day that they gave these people airtime.

When I heard that the pastor of a famous church began teaching hyper-grace a few years ago, I was sick in my heart. I know the church well. But somehow the new pastor became convinced of hyper-grace teaching. At the heart of hyper-grace teaching is the belief that there is no need to confess your sins—no place of repentance is in order in the Christian life; all sins are already forgiven and washed away by Jesus's blood at the cross. Such a teaching will *almost certainly* encourage sexual promiscuity. There have indeed been reports of affairs in some of those churches where this is preached. Mind you, there are similar situations in churches that would abominate hyper-grace, and they too see their share of licentious living. But my point is such sins should be confessed!

King David was a man after God's own heart (1 Sam. 13:14; Acts 13:22). But after David fell, he confessed his sin and repented:

> Have mercy on me, O God,
>   according to your steadfast love;
> according to your abundant mercy
>   blot out my transgressions.
> Wash me thoroughly from my iniquity
>   and cleanse me from my sin!
>
> For I know my transgressions,
>   and my sin is ever before me.
> Against you, you only, have I sinned
>   and done what is evil in your sight,
> so that you may be justified in your words
>   and blameless in your judgment.
>   —PSALM 51:1–4

But that is the old covenant, say the hyper-grace people, and it is therefore not relevant for us who are under the new covenant.

I have seen YouTube clips of a hyper-grace pastor's wife

scantily clad, sensually dancing in the church service. The rationale from this seeker-friendly leadership was that such entertainment would get more people to come to church! No doubt. But to come to church for what? It would only be to hear of "another Jesus"—"a different gospel" (2 Cor. 11:4).

Paul the apostle introduced Romans by the phrase "obedience of faith" with regard to the Gospel (Rom. 1:5). Obedience is part of the Gospel package, if I may put it like that. Obedience is what leads to holy living and to our inheritance—a teaching that the hyper-grace people do not seem to recognize at all. Our inheritance, should we come into it, is what belongs to salvation (Heb. 6:9).

But hyper-grace teaching tells us that obedience is out of the question on our part; we are saved entirely by grace alone through faith alone. That sounds brilliant. In fact, the first hearing of this teaching sounds *so* good. But it is not good. It is bad. Why? It leaves out large chunks of the Bible, especially what the New Testament teaches about reward or inheritance.

We are saved by grace. Grace alone. Faith alone. "For by grace you have been saved through faith. And this is not your own doing; it is the gift of God, not a result of works, so that no one may boast" (Eph. 2:8–9). Grace is unmerited favor, getting what we don't deserve. Grace comes to us from God, who is "rich in mercy" (Eph. 2:4). Mercy is *not* getting what we *do* deserve—judgment. We have no right to boast if we are saved—it is by sheer grace. We praise God in this life and in the life to come.

So can grace be exaggerated? "Probably not," said my late friend and theologian Michael Eaton. "But it can be twisted."[1] And that is what these people do. It is called *hyper-grace* because it draws unwarranted conclusions—using fleshly logic to prove their teaching. They cannot do this without throwing out huge portions of holy Scripture. This to me is at the bottom of the most critical problem: a denial of the full inspiration of the entire Bible.

Much of what hyper-grace teaches smacks of some of the teachings of Marcion, to whom I referred earlier. You may recall that he was said to be the first in the early church to understand Paul but that he also "misunderstood" him. Marcionism was one of the ancient heresies that was antinomian to the core. Marcion was the first to separate the New Testament from the Old Testament. Marcion rejected the God of the Old Testament as wrathful—a tyrant. Such a God was beneath the God of the New Testament. Yahweh was not the same God as spoken by Jesus. Marcion in particular rejected the Epistle to the Hebrews and the pastoral epistles (1 and 2 Timothy; Titus; and Philemon).[2] These are the very same epistles that the hyper-grace people will have nothing to do with.

If I didn't know differently, strange as this may seem, I would also say that hyper-grace doctrine could be traced to some of the teaching of Karl Barth (1886–1968), to whom I will refer in a later chapter. It is carrying grace alone to an extreme that the New Testament writers would find unrecognizable.

Here is the basic teaching of hyper-grace: Jesus did everything for us on the cross. Everything. Our sins are washed away by the blood of Jesus Christ—past, present, future. So far, so good. But since all our sins are totally forgiven by Christ's blood, there is no need to confess them if we sinned. Why confess what has been forgiven already at the cross? That is the logic. It is *hyper-grace*, something accentuated, heightened, and carried to an unthinkable extreme by distorted logic. What those who embrace this teaching do not realize is that it wipes out any basis for intimacy with God and coming into one's inheritance. As we will see in more detail to follow, every Christian is called to come into his or her inheritance. Some do; some don't. Such teaching is utterly absent with the hyper-grace teachers.

When you quote certain scriptures to these people—1 John, Hebrews, or James—the reply is that such books should not be in the canon of Scripture. Sounds like the ancient Marcion to me. They come up with their own canon yet equally have trouble with every single one of the books they accept! As for the Lord's Prayer, which includes the petition "Forgive us our debts, as we also have forgiven our debtors" (Matt. 6:12), that was given before Jesus died on the cross—which makes it irrelevant now. Jesus's teachings were only relevant in His own day! How sad that people would rob you and me of the privilege of praying the Lord's Prayer! Indeed, they pick and choose from Jesus's teachings since they were said before Pentecost. Yet there are some good and sincere people who are lapping up this teaching today. I hate to think of their end. I wonder if they will finish well.

As for the Book of Revelation, that too is disdained by hyper-grace people. Remember Jesus's letters to the seven churches in Asia (Revelation 2–3). Throughout this awesome book our Lord demolishes what would be hyper-grace teaching right, left, and center.

According to Michael Eaton, the hyper-grace people make four mistakes:[3]

1. They say it is wrong to confess our sins. When David said, "I have sinned," having been exposed by Nathan the prophet (2 Sam. 12:13), David made a mistake in saying this. But it is old covenant in any case.

2. As we observed already, the hyper-grace people must throw out huge chunks of the Bible.

3. A Christian must not be given a command from God. This might make us feel guilty, and we should never feel guilty. Even to teach that we should pray and read our Bibles is putting one "under the law."

4. The hyper-grace people forget that we are children of Abraham! After all, God said to Abraham, "Walk before me, and be blameless" (Gen. 17:1).

Eaton added that the hyper-grace people cause justification to "swallow up sanctification."[4] These preachers don't make a distinction between our position in Christ and our call to sanctification (1 Thess. 4:3). According to Paul, whom the hyper-grace people choose to ignore, justification is what *enables* one to demonstrate holy living. Yet Michael Eaton reminded us that holy living is not "automatic"; this is why Paul wrote Ephesians 4 through 6! And

I would add it is why Paul wrote Romans 12 through 16! And Galatians 5 and 6!

The hyper-grace people make no room for Paul's urgency that we should hope for a reward at the judgment seat of Christ (1 Cor. 9:27; 2 Cor. 5:10). They will not deal with verses that say we should try to please the Lord (Eph. 5:10). They totally ignore the doctrine of chastening (Heb. 12:6–13) and, as I said, never take into account the Christian's call to inheritance—which is largely what the Epistle to the Hebrews is about. The New Testament teaching of reward and inheritance is not remotely on the hyper-grace radar screen. Those who accept this teaching are like children playing with an African green mamba.

FURTHER PERSONAL TESTIMONY

I was secretly sympathetic with Charismatics for some twenty years or more because I spoke in tongues spontaneously before telling it to anyone. It came when speaking in tongues was not widely accepted (except in Pentecostal churches), nor was it remotely on my mind. It came to me with a sudden sense of God's presence. It happened to me in February 1956. I suddenly felt a keen sense of God. There was something in me—like in my stomach—that was like a well that wanted to erupt. The only way for it to come out was to speak in what I can only call unintelligible sounds. Others were with me in the car. I was embarrassed. Nobody said a word. I realized I had just spoken in tongues. I told virtually nobody this until I related it to Dr. Martyn Lloyd-Jones in 1977. I feared rejection by anybody who might hear about this. But he assured me that he believed this was a genuine experience of the Holy Spirit. As I report in my book *Holy Fire*, I did not speak in tongues when I was baptized with the Spirit, on October 31, 1955.[5] This came some four months later.

A year or two before retiring from the Westminster pulpit, in 2002, I wondered what I would do when returning to the United States, where I was very unknown. I said to myself, "I will become a recluse and fish twenty-four hours a day in Key Largo." In that moment—barely a second later—it was as real as if it were an audible voice: "Your ministry in America will be to Charismatics." My heart sank. Oh no, please. But it has pretty much turned out that way—all without my turning a hand. Along with other ministry, I was offered a writing platform by Charisma House. And now this book. At age eighty-two I don't know how many years I have left or how many books inside me will see the light of day. But I regard the present book as very timely and pray that God will use it to wake up sleeping Christians of all denominations.

OPEN THEISM

So when at my farewell service at Westminster Chapel I raised the question "Whatever happened to the Gospel?" it was because I had become concerned that many Christian leaders were being lured away from the historic Gospel. A famous Christian theologian was invited to come to London to champion the view called "open theism." I knew what it was: process theology in evangelical dress. I was taught it at seminary. Process theology is one step away from atheism. It is pantheism—*all nature is God*. Some want to call it *panentheism*—with little, if any, difference—meaning that all is *in* God. Some of my professors at Southern Baptist Seminary, in the days before it returned to orthodoxy, believed it and taught it. I could see what this theologian was bringing to London. Never in my life had I asked to speak at a conference. But I asked to speak at this one. The leader of it said yes. But a week or two later the committee said no. I knew that this teaching was deadly and I would even say sub-Christian. But some of my friends were excited by this. I was horrified. The conference came, and many went. At the conference someone asked this well-known theologian this question: "If what you say is true, is it not possible that God could lose and evil would win in the end?" Answer: Yes. The theologian did not think it would end up like that, but yes, that is possible. Amazing. Does this sound like the end of the Book of Revelation to you?

For those who do not know, *open theism* contains the belief that God does not know the future but is open to us—His children—for input in order to know what to do next. God does nothing independently of us; He is dependent upon us for wisdom and for the future. He is "enriched" by His creation. It is the polar opposite of the biblical teaching of the sovereignty of God. But some of my best friends were taking it on board.

FAMOUS IN HELL

One of my mentors—Rolfe Barnard (1904–1969)—used to preach a sermon he titled "The Man Who Was Known in Hell." The sermon was based upon the text "Jesus I know, and Paul I recognize, but who are you?" (Acts 19:15). This is what demons shouted back to some people who thought casting out demons "in the name of Jesus, whom Paul preaches" was a game. They found it was not a game. But Rolfe's point was those who were trying to cast out demons were *not known in hell* (Greek: *tartarus*, used in 2 Pet. 2:4). But the demons certainly knew who Jesus was, and they knew about Paul. The gist of Rolfe's sermon was this: "I want to be known in Hell."

That's me. I would rather be famous in Hell than famous on this planet. I fear I am barely known, if at all, in the satanic world. I would like to think that I was giving the devil so much trouble that I got famous in Hell.

If you should ask how strongly I believe what I write in this book, I would answer, "It is what I am willing to die for." This is because what I write in this book is exactly what the apostle Paul expounds in his letters—particularly Romans and Galatians. I would echo what he says:

> But even if we or an angel from heaven should preach to you a gospel contrary to the one we preached to you, let him be accursed.
> —GALATIANS 1:8

Most people ask, "What's in it for me?" when they go to church or listen to preaching on television.

I hope to demonstrate in the following pages why you should ask, "What's in it for God?"

CHAPTER FIVE

UNASHAMED OF THE GOSPEL

For I am not ashamed of the gospel, for it is
the power of God for salvation to everyone who
believes, to the Jew first and also to the Greek.
—ROMANS 1:16

SHORTLY AFTER I began our ministry at Westminster Chapel, I noticed there were no Gospel tracts in the backs of the pews, only Bibles and hymnals. I decided to write a tract. I called it "What is Christianity?" and gave it to Peter, one of our deacons, to have printed. A few weeks later he phoned.

"The printer says you have made a mistake in your tract, and I should tell you that he is a Christian." I knew instantly what the *mistake* would be! I asked the deacon to continue.

"You say in this tract that Christianity is concerned mostly about your *death*."

"Yes," I agreed.

"Our printer—and he is a Christian, Dr. Kendall—says you should say that Christianity is concerned primarily with your *life*."

"Get another printer, Peter; this is why I am in London."

There has been a widespread consensus among many Christians that the Christian faith is valid even if there were no life to come. Some say, "If there were no Heaven and no Hell, I would still be a Christian."

I know what they mean by that. The Christian faith changes lives on earth and final destinies regarding the age to come. It often gives people a measure of happiness on earth they never had before. But not always, as we will see later.

The question is, Why be a Christian? Do you believe your friends and loved ones should become Christians? If so, why? Does your neighbor need to be a Christian? Does your boss need to be a Christian? Does the Buddhist need to be saved? The Muslim? Why do people need to hear the Gospel of Jesus Christ and embrace it?

I will revisit these questions.

THE MEANING OF
THE WORD *GOSPEL*

The word *gospel* in the Greek language is not inherently Christian or even theological. It was a secular word: *euaggelion*, found seventy-six times in the New Testament and simply meaning "good news."[1] In classical Greek an *euaggelios* was a messenger who announced a victory of personal news that brought joy.

The main thing is what the apostle Paul means by the Gospel when he says, "I am not ashamed of the gospel."

I honestly wonder if some Christians are ashamed of what Paul means by the Gospel as he articulates it in letters such as Romans and Galatians. I am afraid some may be ashamed of it. For there is a great stigma to the Gospel that Paul espouses. It is so offensive. It is why Paul suffered persecution (Gal. 5:11; 6:13–14). But the notion of the blood of Christ pacifying God's justice and wrath in order that we might not go to Hell is most offensive.

Once you know you are going to Heaven, you are *called to enter into your inheritance*. But we need to get the right order. The Gospel first, inheriting the kingdom second. We, through much tribulation, must enter the kingdom of God (Acts 14:22). We don't get to Heaven by going through tribulation; it is by sheer grace. But entering into our inheritance comes through suffering, self-denial, and holiness. What is most important is that you go to Heaven when you die. After all, even if we are healed, we are going to die. What happens when you die is surely more important than being healed.

When I ask, "Whatever happened to the Gospel?" do I mean what some Charismatics call the "gospel of salvation"? Yes, and I am not ashamed of it.

The Gospel is mainly about your death. And some people are, sadly, more interested in their lives than they are in their souls—where they spend eternity. This emphasis in the here and now is, as I said before, called *existentialism*. It is about our "existence"—living in the here and now.

If you ask, "Why do the Gospels refer to the Good News of the 'kingdom'?" it is because Jesus was demonstrating His authority and dominion over the devil in this present world. He had authority over demons and diseases and proved it. It was because He healed on the Sabbath day all the time—which got Him into trouble and which led to His death. His death fulfilled the Law (Matt. 5:17; John 19:30) and became the basis for the Gospel as Paul expounded it.

But when Paul uses *euaggelion* near the beginning of his longest and possibly most important epistle, he merely says: "I am not ashamed of the gospel" (Rom. 1:16). By around AD 60, when Paul wrote Romans, the word *gospel* had probably become for many part of their Christian vocabulary. It became the language of Zion. Paul knew that his readers would know what he meant by saying, "I am not ashamed of the gospel." Some ancient manuscripts indicate that he wrote, "I am not ashamed of the gospel of Christ," as in the King James Version. But the very earliest manuscripts merely state: "I am not ashamed of the gospel." Just the Gospel. The Good News.

Being "unashamed" means you are not afraid of or embarrassed by the stigma—or of being stigmatized because of the Gospel. The word *stigma* is a pure Greek word. It originally was used to describe runaway slaves; they would be given a mark with a hot iron so they would be visibly stigmatized. You and I should never be ashamed of the stigma of upholding the Gospel. Perhaps the word that comes the nearest to *ashamed* is being *embarrassed*. When I first started handing out tracts and speaking to passersby on the steps of Westminster Chapel in Buckingham Gate, the street that runs into Buckingham Palace two blocks away, I admit that I found it a little embarrassing. It was far, far easier to preach in a Geneva gown (which I wore in those days) to hundreds than to approach a complete stranger and ask him if he knows for sure he will go to Heaven when he dies. But when I realized it is something Paul would have done, I soon got over it; he witnessed in the marketplace with those who "happened to be there" (Acts 17:17).

SALVATION—BEING "SAVED"

So what Paul says near the beginning of this most extraordinary epistle is merely, "I am not ashamed of the gospel." For his letter to the Romans is not really about miracles or healing. This is why he immediately adds: "it is the power of God for *salvation*" (emphasis added). That is the key word: *salvation*. This is why Jesus came: "He will *save* his people from their sins" (Matt. 1:21, emphasis added). This is why He died on the cross: "Since, therefore, we have now been justified by his blood, much more shall we be *saved* by him from the wrath of God" (Rom. 5:9, emphasis added). "Brothers, my heart's desire and prayer to God for them is that they may be *saved*" (Rom. 10:1, emphasis added).

We should never be ashamed of the word *saved*. That word for some may have become a little too old-fashioned, and they prefer to use the word *committed* when it comes to their being Christians. This is not a bad word, especially when the distinction needs to be made between those who label themselves "Christian" but never read their Bibles or go to church. But *saved* is the biblical word.

THE WORD *CHRISTIAN*

The word *Christian* too has taken on various meanings. It was originally a derisive term, first applied to believers in Antioch (Acts 11:26). The word had become so known that King Agrippa asked Paul, "In a short time would you persuade me to be a Christian?" (Acts 26:28). The answer is *yes*, Paul tried his best because he *did* think that God could save Agrippa then and there.

Peter urged people not to be ashamed of suffering for the name Christian (1 Pet. 4:16). You and I must be unashamed of the word Christian. Jews and Gentiles should embrace this lovely word unashamedly. I would lovingly urge Jews who come to Christ in faith, who sometimes like to call themselves followers of "Yeshua," equally not to be ashamed of being called a Christian. True, the word has become very common. People will call themselves "Christian" on passports (vis-à-vis Muslim or Buddhist). This would partly justify the term *committed Christian* to those who take the Gospel seriously.

I use the term *Christian* in this book to describe one who has unashamedly embraced the Gospel.

I do not want the Gospel of Jesus Christ to be stigmatized. Neither do I want to be ashamed of words mostly used in Scripture.

The Gospel Is "the Power of God for Salvation"

The word for power here comes from the Greek *dunamis*, from which we get the word *dynamite*. *Dunamis* is often connected to the power of the Holy Spirit; this is what the disciples were told to wait for after Jesus went back to Heaven (Luke 24:49; Acts 1:8). It is the power of the Spirit that heals. It is the power of the Spirit that sets one free from the demonic. It is the power of the Holy Spirit that brings healing, miracles, signs, and wonders.

But that is not what Romans is really about. The Book of Romans was written by a man who had been on his way to arrest, if not to kill, Christians. The last thing Saul of Tarsus dreamed of was being struck to the ground by the power of God. John Wesley said that "God does nothing but in answer to prayer."[2] That is not always true. I do wonder if any of the disciples was literally praying for Saul of Tarsus to be saved. In any case, what stopped Saul in his tracks was power. The explanation for the success of the disciples on the Day of Pentecost is power. The explanation for your conversion and mine is power. There is no other explanation. This is why a Christian is one who is surprised that he or she is a Christian.

Romans therefore is Paul's unfolding of the Gospel that *saves* people—making them fit for Heaven. This is why the Gospel of Christ is the power of God for *salvation*. Whether you and I go to Heaven or Hell when we die is directly and inseparably connected to whether we embrace the Gospel. I will say it again; you could be healed but be lost in Hell. You could see or experience a sign or wonder and be eternally lost.

HEAVEN OR HELL

Does it surprise you that I would write about Heaven and Hell? Whereas I must not apologize for writing like this, I do sympathize if this is new to you. What a pity that no one has told you! If you ask me, "Do you like this teaching?" my answer will be *no*. If God were to leave the matter to me, I would save everybody and do away with Hell. But it is not my idea. Hell is God's idea.

Ludwig Feuerbach (1804–1872) said that God is nothing but man's projection upon the backdrop of the universe.[3] God does not really exist, says Feuerbach; He is the creation of our minds—we *want* to believe that there is someone up there who will look after us and take us to Heaven when we die. Given that rationale, I ask, Whoever would have conceived the idea of Hell? Who wanted that to be true? No human being would come up with such a notion. No sane human being on earth wants to believe Hell exists.

Yet it makes me wonder what the hearers of John the Baptist must have thought when they first heard him speak. The first message recorded in the New Testament refers to the preaching of John the Baptist, who asked his hearers, "Who warned you to flee from the wrath to come?" (Matt. 3:7). Someone should have warned them. Had they heard about coming wrath before? This question implies that probably *no one* had warned them. But John knew what he would have to say to them.

We are in a generation in which virtually no one is warning the world of the wrath of God to come. Hell is at best a swear word today. Or someone will say, "It will be a cold day in Hell when I do this." Therefore when someone does speak as I am writing in this book, it may come as a shock. Some no doubt find it repulsive. Some may roar with laughter and say it is hilarious. For few believe it nowadays. I therefore am not unaware of the work cut out for me when I write like this. Yet you will be convinced *only if the Holy Spirit gets involved* in these lines and causes you to see this is a no-joke matter. The Holy Spirit got involved in the preaching of John the Baptist. The result was that, rather than being put off, hundreds and hundreds of people walked—or came on camels—twenty miles to hear him, from Jerusalem to the desert near the Dead Sea. Should the Holy Spirit come alongside you as you read these lines, you too will not be able to shirk it. The result will be that you are convicted of your sins and your unbelief.

Keep in mind that you will be utterly alone when you stand before God one day. You won't have peer pressure then to influence you, as may be what often motivates you now. This is a matter between you and your Creator. He made you. You are no accident. His eye has been on you since before you were born. It is not by "luck" or chance that you are reading this book; it is the finger of God on your life. You will indeed stand *alone* before God after you die. The most important (and kind) question anybody can put to you is, "Where will you be one hundred years from now?" That is the first question I put to Yasser Arafat (1929–2004), the late president of the Palestinians, when I met with him in Ramallah a few years ago. "Rais, where will you be one hundred years from now? It won't matter then whether you or the Israelis get Jerusalem, but *where will you be*?" As it happened, not only did he not throw me out, but he invited me back. I visited him five times— always praying with him. I will not be surprised to see him in Heaven.

This is why Christianity is primarily concerned about your death! How you respond to the Gospel of Christ will be the *only* thing that matters one hundred years from now.

Paul was unashamed of this Gospel. He was unashamed of the reason people should be saved—because of the coming wrath of God.

That is primarily why Jesus died on the cross. The death of Jesus and the reason He came was so we might go to Heaven and not to Hell. Martin Luther called it "the Bible in a nutshell"[4]—"For God so loved the world, that he gave his only Son, that whoever believes in him should not perish but have eternal life" (John 3:16).

WHO GOES TO HELL?

That is not all. You could be famous and be forever lost in Hell. You could be rich and be lost in Hell. You could be aristocratic or royal and be forever lost in Hell. You could be a genius and be lost in Hell. You can be highly educated and be lost in Hell forever and ever. You could win a Nobel Prize for peace and lose your soul forever. You could believe yourself to be living the best kind of Christian life and go to Hell. You could invent things that will change people's lives for the good—and become world-famous for it—but still go to Hell. You could be beautiful or handsome and become a movie star or rock star and spend eternity in Hell. There is more. You could be poor and go to Hell. You could be an invalid and go to Hell. You could be handicapped—be blind or deaf—and be lost forever. In other words, you could be happy throughout your life—or be unhappy throughout your life—and still lose your soul.

What makes the difference between spending eternity in Heaven or Hell? The Gospel and your response to it.

THE BOOK OF ROMANS

Martin Luther called Romans the "purest Gospel."[5] It is Paul's longest epistle. Why so long, especially when compared with Galatians, which is often referred to as the "little book of Romans"? Luther actually preferred Galatians, preaching through it three times. Virtually all that is in Romans is implicit in his letter to the Galatians, although Galatians can at times be more explicit than Romans (for example, Galatians 2:16, as we will see later). In any case, Romans is his longest letter because first, there was no apostolic leadership in Rome, and Paul felt not only a certain liberty but also an obligation to write to the believers there. Christianity in Rome almost certainly grew not from having been evangelized there but because of the zeal of those Jews who had been converted in Jerusalem on the Day of Pentecost (Acts 2:10). These Jews went to Jerusalem annually to keep the Feast of Pentecost. They were not expecting to return home with a new faith that came from Peter's sermon! They apparently began a church in Rome but without apostolic leadership. Therefore Paul felt free to write to them as he did. Second, as F. F. Bruce says, Paul envisaged going to Rome and wanted them to know exactly what he believed about the Gospel before he got there. It is therefore his most complete statement of the Gospel.[6]

I have preached on Romans 1:16 several times and usually title the sermon "Paul's Confidence in the Gospel."

I bring in Romans 15:20 alongside Romans 1:16, which shows further why Paul is "unashamed":

> I make it my ambition to preach the gospel, not where Christ has already been named, lest I build on someone else's foundation.
> —ROMANS 15:20

> For I am not ashamed of the gospel, for it is the power of God for salvation to everyone who believes, to the Jew first and also to the Greek.
> —ROMANS 1:16

I'm afraid many people entering the ministry today hope to find a settled living awaiting them—a nice place to live, a comfortable home with a white picket fence (or something like that). The thought of going where Jesus Christ is unknown is too challenging for some. They prefer to preach to the choir, as it were, from the first day. Not Paul. He had so much confidence in the *power* of the Gospel that he was not the slightest bit intimidated by people who had never heard of Jesus. Today he would say, "Give me the Muslim. The Buddhist. The atheist. Anyone belonging to a cult." Why? It is because the Gospel is "the power of God for salvation." The assumption in this phrase is the faithfulness of the Holy Spirit to apply the Word. Paul knows that no one *can* come to Christ unless drawn by the Father—which means the Holy Spirit is at work (John 6:44, 65). Paul knows that any conversion is the sovereign work of the Holy Spirit. It is incumbent on him therefore to preach the message that the Holy Spirit will get involved with!

PILOT LIGHTS

During our twenty-five years at Westminster Chapel I invited Arthur Blessitt, the man who has carried a cross around the world, to preach for us. He turned us upside down. One of the fruits of his ministry was the founding of our street ministry—called Pilot Lights. (Please see my chapter on Arthur Blessitt in *In Pursuit of His Glory.*[7]) I led some thirty or more people every week to witness on the streets between Victoria, Big Ben, and Buckingham Palace. Beginning in June 1982 I was personally on the steps of the chapel every Saturday for about two hours, talking to passersby. The early days were extremely difficult. I began to wonder if such a venture was biblical. What set me free was reading Acts 17:17, which states that the great apostle Paul witnessed for Jesus Christ "in the marketplace every day with those who happened to be there." I never looked back after I read this. I said that if Paul could do it, so could I. He was not ashamed to do this, so why should I be ashamed, although we received a lot of criticism (almost entirely from chapel people, not the people to whom we witnessed). During the first three or four years we saw a modest number of people apparently come to Christ, although we never knew for sure who was truly converted and who may have courteously prayed to receive Him.

But there was one Saturday morning, the first Saturday in January 1986, when it was *so* cold and only a half dozen turned up for Pilot Lights. I decided then and there to shut down this ministry. I rehearsed what I would say to the chapel. It went something like this: "We are happy for our

Pilot Lights ministry. It has done us no harm, and we are thankful for the good that has been done. But all good things come to an end, and we will now move on to something else." I planned to make that little speech the next day. Not ten seconds passed when someone rather urgently said, "A man here needs to talk to someone."

I went to him and asked, "Do you want to talk with me?"

"I need to talk with someone about this tract someone gave me last Saturday," he said.

"I wrote that tract," I replied.

"Are you the same Dr. Kendall who wrote this pamphlet, 'What Is Christianity'?"

"Yes."

"My name is Charlie Stride. I am a taxi driver," he said as he pointed to his taxi. "One of your lads gave me this last Saturday. I have thrown away a thousand of these, but for some reason I read this as I waited in a taxi line last Saturday. Could I ask you some questions?"

"Certainly. Why don't we sit in your taxi?" I was thinking how nice this would be, seeing how cold it was!

"This tract shook me rigid," he began. "But I need to make sure I have understood this. Will I go to Hell if I don't become a Christian?"

"I'm afraid you will, Charlie."

"But many of my fellow taxi drivers are Jews. Will they too go to Hell?"

"I don't know, but if they don't receive Christ, they will."

I thought he would end the conversation and ask me to get out of the taxi, but he didn't. He was in tears.

"Charlie, can I go over the things written in this tract with you?"

"Oh, please do," he said.

I presented the Gospel to him then asked if he would like to pray the prayer with me that is at the end of the pamphlet.

"Yes, please."

Charlie Stride prayed the prayer and was instantly converted. He came to Westminster Chapel the next day. I did *not* make that speech about closing down the Pilot Lights ministry. I was out on the streets on Saturdays with the Pilot Lights until we retired. Charlie Stride's conversion came in the nick of time. God knew how much I needed encouragement. Truly, God is never too late, never too early, but always just on time. The Pilot Lights ministry therefore kept going. It still continues!

One day Benjamin Chan, one of our deacons, asked if he could lead a prayer meeting on Saturday mornings during the time our Pilot Lights were out on the streets witnessing. That little prayer meeting only included six or seven faithful intercessors. But something extraordinary took place almost immediately after these Saturday morning prayer meetings began. Whereas up until then we might have had one or two to pray to receive Christ from time to time, we began seeing six, eight, ten, or twelve pray *every week*. Were they all converted? Only God knows. One of them, reportedly, went into the Anglican ministry. I have had people from all over the UK come up to me to thank me for the blessing of the Pilot Lights ministry. An Anglican vicar came to hear me preach in the Midlands because he wanted to tell me that our Pilot Lights ministry brought his own daughter to the Lord. A man on the staff of an event called Spring Harvest came up to me to say I had led him to the Lord on the steps of Westminster Chapel. After retiring, I received a letter from Germany. A lady wrote that she had prayed for her father for years to be saved. She said I gave her a tract in front of Westminster Chapel—translated into German. Because the tract was in German, her father agreed to read it. He prayed the prayer at the end of the tract. He died the next day.

Within a few weeks of praying to receive Christ in the back seat of his taxi, Charlie Stride asked to be baptized. After several months he asked if he could join the church. Charlie became our most popular member! He was active with our young people and learned how he himself could lead people to the Lord. He became a soul winner.

I had been wanting to ask Charlie for years about the tract—and what it was that gripped him. "It was that part about death," he said. "That is what *shook me rigid*." I told him that I was asked to change "death" to "life" in that pamphlet. He said to me that he would have kept reading it without any effect had it said that Christianity is mainly concerned with one's "life."

It was one of the sweetest vindications I have ever had.

At the farewell service for us, to which I referred at the beginning of this book, several prominent people spoke and said nice things about me. Among them: J. John, Richard Bewes, Sandy Millar, and Sir Fred Catherwood. To my surprise Lyndon Bowring asked Charlie Stride to speak. Charlie stole the show! He told the story virtually verbatim as I outlined above. It was the icing on the cake on a memorable evening.

After we retired, Charlie, who had been a widower,

married a lovely lady from the Philippines who had become a member of the chapel. Shortly after we retired, he too retired. He and his wife moved to the Philippines. I heard he became ill. I phoned him. His voice was weak. I prayed for him during that phone call for the last time. He died the next day.

When Arthur Blessitt was with us during the month of May 1982, I walked around with him as he talked to *anyone*—literally the next person we ran into—about Jesus Christ. He became a mentor in so many ways. It was his witnessing to three young people in front of the chapel one Friday evening that led me to the Pilot Lights ministry. When I saw a vision of a pilot light—like in a cooker or oven—that stays lit day and night, I died a thousand deaths because it seemed that my ambitions, plans, and wishes to be a great theologian at His feet in ashes lay.

It is a lot harder to talk to one person than it is to preach to thousands. After Arthur went to his next appointment after spending several weeks with us, I began the Pilot Lights ministry. I was nervous. Embarrassed? Ashamed? No, but very conscious that so many respected members of the chapel were against this venture. But each week got easier and easier. Arthur's anointing was in some ways passed on to me. I can tell you that I have led hundreds and hundreds of people to pray to receive Jesus Christ—in Buckingham Gate, in barbershops, on planes, in restaurants, and in people's homes.

I had never done anything like this, witnessing to strangers, in my life. But reading Acts 17:17 about Paul witnessing to anybody in the marketplace gave me the assurance to talk to people about Jesus in the streets. I use the Evangelism Explosion method, designed by the late D. James Kennedy. We ask these two questions:

1. Do you know for sure that if you were to die today, you would go to Heaven?

2. If you were to stand before God, which you will, and He were to ask you, which He might, "Why should I let you into My Heaven?" what would you say?

You, the reader, need to focus on these same two questions. What would be your answers?

I did my very best to get all of the Gospel that I possibly could in my words when talking to passersby. I knew we would possibly never meet again. I would speak to them as if their destiny was in my hands. I sought to focus on Jesus Christ, the God-man, and His death on the cross as the only way to be saved.

The Holy Spirit only anoints the truth. If I want the anointing on my preaching or writing, I need to be sure of at least one thing: what I assert is *true*. Among the profoundest words I ever heard uttered were these by Joni Eareckson Tada, the quadriplegic lady who has so honored God all over the world by her testimony about Jesus Christ: "I am not a Christian because of what it does for me; I am a Christian because it is true."[8] This statement always reminds me of what Charles H. Spurgeon (1834–1892) used to say regarding those who came to learn from him. He said that one cannot teach another "how" to preach, but we can teach them "what to preach."

Content—what you actually say when talking about Jesus Christ—is so important.

My wife, Louise, was not so sure I should be talking to passersby on the streets of London. "You don't have to be Arthur Blessitt," she would say. True. And possibly not everybody can do that. However, Louise decided one Saturday morning that she would join the Pilot Lights. I was surprised. She said later that she asked God for a sign that she should be doing this. Minutes after she began passing out tracts at St. James Park station, a young man wearing a Che Guevara T-shirt came to her. She said nervously to him, "Would you consider reading this tract?"

He read the title back to her, "What is Christianity?" Tears filled his eyes. "I'm a Marxist," he said. "I'm an atheist. But five minutes ago I was in a church, and I said, 'God, if You are really there, let me run into someone who believes in You.'" He took the tract. Louise never saw him again. We have prayed for him many, many times, hoping we will see him in Heaven.

I am not ashamed of the Gospel. Can you say that?

Will you be in Heaven one day? An old spiritual coming out of the cotton fields of Alabama puts it like this: "Not everybody who talks about Heaven is going there."

But will you be there?

The Holy Spirit only anoints the truth, even if you and I can't say everything we would like to say when talking about Jesus Christ. That is why Paul could say, "I am not ashamed of the gospel." *Any part* of the Gospel can be applied effectually by the Holy Spirit and lead to one's conversion. The Gospel is "the power of God for salvation" *because* the mention of the blood of Jesus is what gets the

Holy Spirit involved. He then moves in to convict and to convert.

There is one reason and one reason alone we should be unashamed of the Gospel: *because it is true.*

CHAPTER SIX

THE HEART OF THE GOSPEL

*For all have sinned and fall short of the glory of God,
and are justified by his grace as a gift, through the
redemption that is in Christ Jesus, whom God put
forward as a propitiation by his blood, to be received
by faith. This was to show God's righteousness.... Then
what becomes of our boasting? It is excluded.... To the
one who does not work but believes in him who justifies
the ungodly, his faith is counted as righteousness.*
—ROMANS 3:23–25, 27; 4:5

PRESIDENT RONALD REAGAN kept a plaque on his desk in the Oval Office that read: "There is no limit to the amount of good you can do if you don't care who gets the credit."[1] That said, how far is Heaven? If a person makes it to Heaven, he has gone a long way—indeed, as far as a person can go! When you consider eternity, an existence that lasts forever and ever, making it to Heaven becomes the most important accomplishment you can imagine.

But here's the deal: Heaven is reachable only by those who don't care who gets the credit for it. If you want the credit, forget about going to Heaven. But if you don't care who gets the credit, you qualify to continue this discussion.

We all are made in such a way that we naturally want credit for what we do. God recognizes this throughout Holy Scripture, often appealing to our self-interest to motivate us to do what is best for us. We would naturally like a reward for doing what is unusual or hard. We, by nature, want recognition. Jesus therefore asked the question "If you do good to those who do good to you, what *credit* is that to you?" (Luke 6:33, NKJV, emphasis added). But on that particular occasion Jesus was not talking about how to get to Heaven but how to get your inheritance on your way to Heaven and ensure a reward at the judgment seat of Christ. Our inheritance—what comes to us by persistent faith after we are saved—accompanies salvation (Heb. 6:9).

TWO KINDS OF BIBLICAL FAITH

There are two kinds of faith:

1. saving, justifying faith
2. persistent faith

Justifying faith is what saves us and ensures that we will go to Heaven when we die. Persistent faith is what *follows* saving, or justifying, faith. Justifying faith is what gets you to Heaven. You get no credit for that. But the kind of faith that leads us to our inheritance and brings a reward at the judgment seat of Christ is persistent faith. Persistent faith therefore pertains to the person who is *already assured* of going to Heaven.

This part of my book is about the first kind of faith— saving, or justifying, faith.

Oliver Cromwell (1599–1658) liked to use a phrase, "the heart of the matter," emphasizing what he saw as fundamental in any discussion. So when it comes to the Gospel, one needs to grasp the heart of the matter clearly.

When I talk about going to Heaven, I am using my language to show what justification by faith ultimately leads to: spending eternity with God. Going to Heaven is the *bottom line* as to why it is urgently important that we understand Paul's language. Paul does not speak of going to Heaven but rather of having "eternal life" (Rom. 6:23). He speaks of being justified by the blood of Jesus to escape the coming wrath of God (Rom. 1:18; 5:9). It comes to this: going to Heaven and not to Hell.

THE ISSUE: WHO GETS THE CREDIT?

There are two questions that are relevant here. One is a question *you* may well ask when you hear the Gospel for the first time: "Is this not too good to be true?" And you will likely ask the same question for the rest of your life!

The other is a question Paul asks in order to help us get to the heart of the matter: "Where is boasting?" He asks it because it helps us see more clearly what he is talking about. Regarding the first question, if you say to yourself, "Is this not too good to be true?" it suggests that you are beginning to understand the Gospel. But to make sure you have understood it indeed, Paul asks his question, "Where is boasting?" or "What becomes of our boasting?" (Rom. 3:27). To him it is like what we today call the "elephant in the room"—what people are thinking but don't mention. Paul was a Jew and knew how the Jewish mind works. He knew that the issue of *who gets the credit* was what a Jew would quickly think. The issue of boasting is implicitly right in the middle of his argument, so he raises it. This also helps to peel the layers of the onion, so to speak, in order to get to the heart of the matter.

The answer to Paul's question, "What becomes of our boasting?" is that *boasting is excluded* (v. 27). Boasting is out of the question. Any bragging regarding our being justified in the sight of God is taken right out of our hands. The entire glory goes to God if ever you are declared righteous before Him. What Paul then proceeds to do toward the end of Romans 3 and into Romans 4 is show exactly how it is truly possible that we can be declared righteous in God's sight.

In a word: it is by faith alone in the blood of Christ alone.

Strange as it may seem, what makes the Gospel of Christ so hard to take in but also so offensive is that Heaven is totally a free gift. It is not earned by anything we do. Heaven is not given to you as a reward for being good. It is not given as a reward for anything you do. It is entirely a gift—free. It is hard to take this in because by nature we assume that we must earn our way to Heaven.

I have talked to many atheists when witnessing for Christ. When they say, "I don't believe there is a Heaven," I say to them, "But if there *is* a Heaven—for the sake of argument, what would you say to God if He asks you why He should let you in?"

They *invariably* answer in words such as, "I have tried to be good," "I am not a bad person," "I am good to people," "I have done nothing very bad," or "I have done a lot of good in life." How did they know to answer like that? Where did they learn it? Had they been to Sunday school? To church? No. I am talking about people who know *nothing* about God. Yet they assume that if there is a God and if there is a Heaven, it comes down to one thing: earning it. No one taught them that. We get it by nature. It is part of our natural way of thinking. The Bible calls it *self-righteousness*. People assume that if there is such a thing as Heaven, it will be earned by what we do that is good.

No. It is God's free "gift" (Rom. 3:24; 6:23).

The Jew thought that righteousness before God could only be one's own personal righteousness. Earning your way. Getting credit for reaching a standard. They wanted to establish their *own* righteousness (Rom. 10:3). Therefore the notion of a righteousness from God as a *gift* was utterly alien to their thinking.

It may surprise you that Heaven is a free gift. That is the only way you and I could ever get to Heaven; it is because God *gives it to you.* Here is why: Achieving Heaven requires perfection. Nothing unclean can enter Heaven. Yes, getting to Heaven certainly requires perfection of a person—sixty seconds a minute, sixty minutes an hour, twenty-four hours a day, every day of your life! No person who has the slightest taint of sin can get into Heaven. Neither you nor I am perfect. All have sinned and have fallen short of God's glory. To make this even clearer, Paul says that God justifies "the ungodly," God's "enemies" (Rom. 5:6, 10). He does not justify righteous people; righteous people would not need it. He only justifies wicked people.

And, by the way, is that not the sort of person you really are? Are you godly or ungodly? I have to tell you, if you see yourself as righteous, you are not a candidate for Heaven. I'm sorry, but those who qualify to go to Heaven are those who *admit* what the Bible says is true—that they are *sinners*. Jesus was criticized by the Jews for keeping company with "sinners" (Luke 15:1–2). He said to His critics, "Those who are well have no need of a physician, but those who are sick. I have not come to call the righteous but sinners to repentance" (Luke 5:31–32).

You may ask, "If perfect righteousness is required to get into Heaven, and all of us are sinners, how does anybody ever get into Heaven?"

I answer, "God gives it to you."

How can God do this? God provides a substitute for you. We need a substitute if we are to get to Heaven. Someone who would take our place. Someone who was totally and perfectly righteous in our behalf. Someone who was righteous sixty seconds a minute, sixty minutes an hour, twenty-four hours a day, every day of his life.

That is exactly what Jesus was. He never sinned. He knew no sin. He was your substitute by His perfect, sinless life. But when He died on the cross, He who knew no sin was made sin (2 Cor. 5:21). On Good Friday *all* of our sins were transferred to Jesus. The Lord laid upon Him "the iniquity of us all" (Isa. 53:6). He took the blame for our sins. He was literally our substitute—by His sinless life and His sacrificial death. "In Christ God was reconciling the world to himself, not counting their trespasses against them" (2 Cor. 5:19). This is why we are saved not only by Christ's death but also by His "life" (Rom. 5:10).

Does this sound too good to be true? Do you now see why any boasting on our part is excluded? If you become a millionaire, that is an achievement you can be proud of. You may say, "But I have worked for it." True. Or if you become a politician and run for office—and win— you may say, "But I worked hard to achieve this." If you are a genius and invent a new product—whether it be in computer technology or in aeronautics—you may well say, "I worked for it." If you win the Nobel Prize for peace— a remarkable accomplishment indeed—you may thank people who helped you get there but would equally say, "I paid a high price to receive this—in patience, diplomacy, and hard work." In such cases one would grant you the right to feel a bit proud. You deserve congratulations. You would be forgiven for boasting.

But if you make it to Heaven, you get no credit for it. Not even a little bit. God gets the credit for it all. It is a destiny that is granted to you that nothing else can match. Yet because of this there are actually those who want no part of the true Gospel. They cannot bear the thought of having someone else doing it all for them—without their aid or effort. Consequently many people reject the Gospel. Their self-righteousness and egos prevail. And they lose their souls.

"Salvation is *all of grace*," as Charles Spurgeon put it.[2] Totally of grace. This is why Paul asks the question, to make sure you have truly been following his argument, "What becomes of our boasting? It is excluded" (Rom. 3:27).

WHAT'S IN IT FOR GOD?

I hope you noticed the word *propitiation* above (Rom. 3:25). This is essential to Christ's atonement. There are, in fact, two words you should know: *expiation* and *propitiation*. *Expiation* is "what the blood of Christ does for us"—granting us forgiveness of sins. *Propitiation* is "what the blood of Jesus does for God"—turning His wrath away. It is what satisfies God's justice. That was needed before we could have forgiveness of sins. God's justice was satisfied on Good Friday, when Jesus cried out, "My God, my God, why have you forsaken me" (Matt. 27:46). That was the moment when Jesus, who up to that moment "knew no sin," was "made...to be sin" (2 Cor. 5:21). At some point in time between noon and three o'clock on Good Friday our sins were transferred from us to Jesus. That is precisely when God punished Jesus for what we did. Never forget that Jesus did not die for His own sins; He never sinned at all (Heb. 4:15). He died for *our* sins—the sins *we* committed. *Our sins put Him on the cross.*

Here are two more words that are important for you to know: *substitution* and *satisfaction*. Charles Spurgeon says there is no Gospel apart from these.[3] As we saw, Jesus was our substitute—took our place. He was our substitute by His sinless life; He was our substitute by His death, taking the punishment that we deserved. The blood He shed cried out for justice—satisfaction. God's wrath was appeased by the blood of Jesus Christ. His blood turned God's wrath away.

So often people say, "Why don't you talk about the love of God rather than the wrath of God?" I reply, "This entire discussion is about the love of God! It is the love of God that is at the bottom of the Gospel! It is the love of Jesus Christ for His people that drove Him to the cross."

The motivation to go to the cross came from Jesus Himself—it is what He chose to do. Yet the motivation came from God the Father from before the foundation of the world, the cross being the *reason* He sent His Son, Jesus, into this world in the first place. It is a supremely important teaching that God *sent* His Son into the world (John 3:17). The Son was with the Father from the beginning, when He was the Word (Greek: *logos*, John 1:1). This brings us to the Bible in a nutshell: "God so loved the world, that he gave his only Son"—this being His death on the cross (John 3:16). The Father *sent* the Son, and then on Good Friday He *gave* His Son to die on the cross. God the Father was at the bottom of it all.

To summarize, two things took place simultaneously on Good Friday—the day God punished Jesus for our sins:

1. Our sins were transferred from us to Jesus (2 Cor. 5:21).

2. His righteousness was transferred to us (2 Cor. 5:19).

I reckon that a good way to know whether you have truly understood the Gospel is whether it seems too good to be true. Until it seems too good to be true, chances are you have not grasped it.

Let us say you owe your bank $100,000. You go see your bank manager to tell him that sadly you do not have the $100,000. He looks at your account and notices that someone came to the bank and paid the $100,000 for you. He tells you that your debt has been paid and the bank is no longer looking for money from you. Would you not find this too good to be true? But what if it is true? Would you not be overwhelmed?

Some would say that the Gospel is not "good news" unless you heard "bad news" first. That is sometimes true. G. Campbell Morgan (1863–1945) used to say that it was his experience that people responded to the Gospel more often when the fear of eternal punishment was preached. For example, if you are told, and have been convinced, that you are truly going to Hell but hear that Jesus's death changed this in your behalf, the Gospel truly becomes "Good News" to you. Yet I am sure there are many people who truly come to Christ without having heard of Hell at all. For that reason some ministers never preach on eternal punishment, which is sad.

Yet the Gospel is "Good News" because we are promised Heaven by "faith plus nothing," as Francis Schaeffer (1912–1984) would say.[4] Righteousness is put to the credit to the one who "does not work" but trusts God, who "justifies the ungodly" (Rom. 4:5).

Implicit all along in this book so far is that the Gospel is the Good News that we go to Heaven and not to Hell by relying solely on the blood of Christ and not our good works. The Gospel, in a word, is that we are saved by relying on Christ alone. Relying on His life and His death. Plus nothing.

Yet there is a parallel strain in Romans that would focus on the resurrection of Christ for assurance of salvation. One of the differences between the Eastern Church (e.g. Greek Orthodox, Russian Orthodox) and the Western Church (Protestantism and Roman Catholicism) is that the former emphasizes the resurrection of Jesus; the latter, the death of Christ. In actual sequence the resurrection of Christ comes first in Romans: Jesus was declared to be the Son of God by "his resurrection from the dead" (Rom. 1:4). This also shows that affirming Christ's deity is inseparably joined to the resurrection of Christ. Paul said, "If you confess with your mouth that Jesus is Lord and believe in your heart that God raised him from the dead, you will be saved" (Rom. 10:9). Romans 1:4 shows that the affirmation "Jesus is Lord" in Romans 10:9 is to affirm His deity—that Jesus is the Son of God. This means He is God the Son. Affirming that Jesus is Lord is saying that Jesus is God. No one can say this from the heart except by the Holy Spirit (1 Cor. 12:3).

One could base his or her assurance of salvation either on the death of Jesus or the resurrection of Jesus, that is, if this affirmation is from the "heart." You must believe in your heart that Jesus is God; you must believe in your heart that God raised Jesus from the dead. This removes faith as being merely "assent" as a basis for assurance. "For with the heart one believes and is justified, and with the mouth one confesses and is saved" (Rom. 10:10).

But note too that one *confesses* these truths. This implies what one does in the open. You confess to be seen and heard. People hear your confession. This almost certainly refers to Christian baptism. It is not the baptism itself that saves, however; it is what is in the heart that makes the difference. As St. Augustine (d. 430) put it, "Baptism is an outward sign of an inward work."[5] One is baptized to demonstrate that he or she is unashamed of the Gospel. Even "secret believers" eventually come out of the closet to confess Jesus Christ, such as Nicodemus (John 3:1–8; 19:39) and Joseph of Arimathea (John 19:38). There are countless Muslims today who are secret believers, but they will eventually come out of hiding and reveal their faith.

I would now offer two valid proofs that one has embraced the Gospel. One may call these definitions of *saving faith*. First is my own preferred definition: *saving faith* is "reliance upon Christ's blood alone." Second, it is "believing that Jesus is God who was raised from the dead."

Either of these definitions makes a person fit for Heaven. Either of these definitions guarantees that righteousness has been put to our credit. This may shed light on Luther's previously mentioned three surprises:

1. There will be those we don't expect to see, but they embraced the Good News when they heard it.

2. There will be those not in Heaven because they did not believe the truths this chapter has espoused. They trusted entirely in their personal righteousness.

3. The greatest surprise of all: that he himself is there.

A few years ago, while I was still at Westminster Chapel, Pastor Colin Dye of Kensington Temple and I spent four hours in an Indian restaurant in London discussing theology with a well-known theologian from America. The conversation centered on Paul's teaching of justification by faith. I upheld justification by "faith alone." The American theologian upheld justification by "faith evidenced by works." We were getting nowhere. It was now almost 11:00 p.m. I then asked him: "If you are standing before God at the judgment, on what basis would you rest your own final destiny—trusting Christ's righteousness or your righteousness?"

To my astonishment this man said: "My righteousness." That moment was epoch-making for Colin. It crystallized his own thinking; he never looked back. For me it was an unforgettable confirmation of all I have preached for more than sixty years. I have always known that if a person says you must have faith plus works, when the crunch comes, it is *works* people ultimately trust to assure themselves that they are saved. To be fair, I should tell you that I met with this man since retiring from Westminster Chapel. He seemed to climb down from what he said that night, saying he was in jet lag. I was pleased to hear this.

When it comes time to die, what you truly believe in your heart is what will matter. What really happened on Good Friday is the heart of the matter. Whether you go to Heaven or Hell is the heart of the matter.

CHAPTER SEVEN

THE FAITH OF CHRIST

*For therein is the righteousness of God revealed from
faith to faith: as it is written, The just shall live by faith.*
—ROMANS 1:17, KJV

*Knowing that a man is not justified by the works of
the law, but by the faith of Jesus Christ, even we have
believed in Jesus Christ, that we might be justified by
the faith of Christ, and not by the works of the law:
for by the works of the law shall no flesh be justified.*
—GALATIANS 2:16, KJV

I REMEMBER IT SO well. I drove our son, TR (as we
call him), age eleven, to Montpelier school in Ealing,
London, for his first day there. He would not get out
of the car. This was the fourth school he would be entering
within a period of one year. None of the previous schools
had been pleasant for him, and he could not bear the
thought of starting all over again in a new English school.
I said, "Look at those boys on the playground; they will be
your new friends." He would not budge. The anxiety was
almost as intense for me as it was for him. "TR, you really
do have to go." He stared at the floor, would not move. I

prayed hard to know what to do. "TR, look at me. I will be praying for you nonstop *all day long.* When you get nervous, remember, Daddy is praying for you. When you feel afraid, whatever time of the day it is, know that I am praying for you. *All day long nonstop—remember I am praying for you.*"

It worked. He opened the car door, walked onto the playground without looking back. It wasn't his faith that got him moving; it was my promise to pray for him that did it. He knew he could live that day by *my* faithfulness to pray for him without any letup. I don't know whether he himself prayed much that day or had much faith of his own, but one thing was for sure: he was counting on my praying for him. He was living that day by *my* faithfulness and my faith.

That was the first time I had applied my teaching about the faith of Jesus Christ in such a practical way. In my own Christian walk I had learned to live by Christ's faithfulness to pray for me at the Father's right hand with a perfect faith. The first time I became acutely aware of Christ's faith and faithfulness was on October 31, 1955, when I perceived Jesus to be interceding for me at the right hand of God. While at Oxford I wrote a little chorus. I taught it to my church in Lower Heyford, Oxfordshire, and later shared it with Westminster Chapel:

> I live by the faith of the Son of God,
> I live by the faith of the Son of God
> Who lived and died and rose again
> And prays for me at the Father's right hand.

He prays for me at the Father's right hand,
He prays for me at the Father's right hand
With perfect faith and perfect love
He brings my need to the Father above.

WHY IS THIS CHAPTER SO IMPORTANT?

Could the teaching of this chapter be new to you? If so, why is it so important that I devote an entire chapter to the faith of Christ? The answer is because it is fundamental to Paul's doctrine of justification by faith. It causes all his arguments to cohere and make sense. Most importantly it shows that there is nothing meritorious in *our* faith. Our faith is but the instrument that puts the promise and revelation of the righteousness of God into effect. Essential though our faith is to be saved, the glory goes entirely to God, and that is why we should extol the glory of the cross. The purpose of this chapter is to show how the *merit* of Jesus's sinless life and faith is the foundation of our justification. The focus is not on our faith but the glory, faith, and faithfulness of Jesus Christ.

Jesus was a man of faith. He was God. He was man. He was and is the God-man. But as a man He was the perfect believer. This is why Paul says we are "saved by his life" (Rom. 5:10). In this book I have mostly focused on Jesus's death. But His death must never be separated from His life. His sinless life. His keeping His promise to fulfill the Law (Matt. 5:17). To complete the work the Father gave Him (John 5:36), which was "finished" on the cross (John 19:30).

When Isaiah said of the coming Messiah, "I will hope in

him" (Isa. 8:17), it was a forecast of Jesus's own faith (Heb. 2:13). As a man Jesus was given the Holy Spirit "without measure" (John 3:34). You and I have the Spirit in measure (Rom. 12:3), but Jesus had the Spirit without measure, without limit. This is why Jesus as a man had perfect faith. As our substitute He did everything that is required of us:

- He kept the Law for us (Matt. 5:17).

- He was baptized for us (Matt. 3:15).

- He believed for us (Gal. 2:16).

- He died for us (Rom. 5:9).

- He was raised from the dead for us (Rom. 4:25).

- He now intercedes for us at the right hand of God the Father (Heb. 7:25).

Thus in the moment we transfer our trust in good works to His work for us, His righteousness is put to our credit—as though we too had done what He did. That is what saves us and guarantees we will go to Heaven when we die.

WHAT DAVID BRAINERD HAD TO ACCEPT BEFORE HE WAS CONVERTED

My old mentor Rolfe Barnard preached a sermon in 1963 on "Four Things That David Brainerd Learned." David Brainerd (1718–1747) was a missionary to the American Indians. He died of tuberculosis at the age of twenty-nine.

Had he lived, he would have become the son-in-law of Jonathan Edwards (1703–1758). Edwards was at Brainerd's side when he died and told how the glory of God came into the room as Brainerd went to Heaven. In 1749 Edwards published the *The Life and Diary of David Brainerd.*[1] This book is frequently said to have motivated more people to go to the mission field than any other work of literature in church history. John Wesley read it and urged, "Let every preacher read carefully over *The Life and Diary of David Brainerd.*"[2]

But Brainerd had a long quarrel with God before he was converted. The more he discovered about God, the more Brainerd hated Him. He first discovered that God demanded perfect righteousness, and Brainerd knew he didn't have it. It meant he had to have a substitute, and this made him angry with God. Second, he discovered that God required a perfect faith, and Brainerd didn't have it. It meant God had to give it to him. This made him all the more angry. But what infuriated him most of all was the realization that God could give faith or withhold it—and be just either way. Finally Brainerd saw that God could save him or damn him—and be just either way.

But God had mercy on David Brainerd and saved him, and he became a legend.

Jesus had a perfect faith. The apostle Paul therefore said, "I live by *the faith* of the Son of God" (Gal. 2:20, KJV, emphasis added). Living by His faith. Our faith is weak. Christ's faith is strong. We live not by our weak, vacillating faith but by His constant, unwavering faith. It means to lean on His faith—or faithfulness.

Some say, "I live by the Golden Rule." Some might say,

"I live by the Ten Commandments." Some might say, "I live by my new diet." Paul said, "I live by the faith [or faithfulness] of the Son of God." He was not relying on his own faithfulness; he relied on Christ's faith, on Christ's keeping the Law and Christ's death on the cross. In a word: it was faith in Christ's faith, or faithfulness.

WHAT LED ME TO A
WONDERFUL BREAKTHROUGH

Although I had come to understand the faith of Christ from the verses I have quoted in this chapter, especially Galatians 2:20, I had never made sense of the phrase "faith to faith" in Romans 1:17 (KJV). My understanding of this verse evolved from my viva voce (oral exam) at Oxford. Sometimes academic examinations are truly learning experiences. But I was not prepared for the breakthrough that would eventually come to me following my oral exam at Oxford in December 1976.

One of my examiners was T. H. L. Parker (1916–2016), a biographer of John Calvin and a highly respected Anglican theologian. Parker was a translator of some of John Calvin's commentaries. He was known also as an ardent devotee of the Swiss theologian Karl Barth (1886–1968), almost certainly the greatest theologian of the twentieth century. I knew a fair bit about Barth, having taken a graduate seminar on his theology at Southern Baptist Theological Seminary. But my Oxford thesis was about Calvin. I never mentioned Barth. At my DPhil viva voce, however, Parker wanted to compare Calvin to Barth. What emerged from the dialogue was Parker's comment:

"Your thesis has shown the difference between Calvin and Barth." Many Barthians have fancied that Karl Barth was a Calvinist; among them almost certainly was Parker. His comment at my viva voce was an honest admission that Barth and Calvin were not so close together after all. That comment implanted a time bomb in me. I began to realize gradually but eventually how significant this was.

The difference was this: Barth believed we are saved by the faith of Christ—that Jesus Christ as our substitute believed perfectly and savingly for all men. We ourselves do not need to believe to be saved; Christ's faith saves us. I got to know Barth's esteemed protégé, Professor Thomas F. Torrance of New College, Edinburgh University. You may recall my reference to Torrance previously. Professor Torrance says that we are not saved by our faith; we are saved by the faith of Christ. What my thesis did for T. H. L. Parker was show that, according to Calvin, we *too* must believe in order to be saved. If you will forgive the anachronism, Calvin was no Barthian! What Parker's comment did for me was cause me to see the meaning of "faith to faith" in Romans 1:17 (KJV).

I don't encourage people to read Karl Barth. Quite the opposite. He has been responsible for luring many a young theological student from sound theology. Few Barthians stay Barthians for long. Nearly all of them that I have known sooner or later discard Barth and often move to thinkers such as Paul Tillich (1886–1965). Being in the Lutheran tradition, Tillich emphasized faith. He defined *faith* as "ultimate concern." He defined God as the "ground of all being." With these definitions an atheist could have faith, and Tillich happily said so.

Whatever happened to the Gospel? Liberalism won the day in the majority of seminaries and faculties of theology in universities in the 1960s—on both sides of the Atlantic. One of my professors at my old seminary was the very same man, ironically, who persuaded me to go to Oxford. I was thinking of going to Edinburgh. On this I am glad I listened to him! He recommended me to the Faculty of Divinity of Oxford University. Yet he said, "I moved from fundamentalism to Barth. I went from Barth to Tillich. From Tillich I went to process theology. And I don't know where I am now."[3]

So many followers of Tillich began with following Karl Barth. Not only do very few Barthians remain Barthians, but what is more is there are no Barthian evangelists. Barthians do not become soul winners. Why should they? According to them, Jesus believed savingly for all, died savingly for all. There is no need to tell them that they too must believe because they are saved whether they believe or not. That is Barthianism. The Gospel to a Barthian is merely telling people the good news that they have *already* been saved—two thousand years ago by Jesus's faith and death.

If Paul could say that he is a debtor to both the wise and the unwise (Rom. 1:14), there is one thing that Karl Barth and Thomas F. Torrance helped me see more clearly, and I will be eternally grateful for this: *the crucial significance of Jesus's own faith.* I had never truly grasped that. Not only that; I began to see that Paul builds his entire doctrine of justification on the faith of Christ. That is what Paul means by the expression "faith to faith." In the Gospel a righteousness is revealed, a righteousness from God that is from *"faith to faith"* (Rom. 1:17): "faith" (Jesus's faith) "to faith" (our faith). His faith saves us; our faith puts it into effect. Christ's faith is the meritorious cause; our faith is the instrumental cause. Christ's faith saves us on the condition that we too believe. Our faith ratifies what Jesus did by His life and death.

THE ABSOLUTE NECESSITY OF OUR OWN FAITH

In a word, Christ's faith must be ratified by our faith, or we will be eternally lost. He believed perfectly for us, yes; but if we ourselves don't also believe, all that Jesus did and suffered for the human race is of "no value" (Calvin's words).[4] That means that people will perish—go to Hell—if they don't believe the Gospel. For God so loved the world that whosoever *believes* on His Son will not perish but have eternal life (John 3:16). If we don't believe, we perish. The New Testament denies universalism.

You will have noticed that the scriptures quoted in this chapter are from the King James Version. The reason: it is the only version I know of that translates the Greek *pistis christou* "faith of Christ." All other versions—even the New King James Version—sadly translate this Greek phrase "faith in Christ." The issue turns on whether *pistis christou* is the objective genitive—faith *in* Christ—or the subjective genitive—faith *of* Christ—that is, Jesus's own faith.

To put it succinctly, "faith to faith" means two faiths that must be completed to save us. The first faith is Christ's; the second is ours. The two together equal salvation.

I have talked personally to some of the translators (whom I deeply respect) of the New International Version and the English Standard Version. Could they not—at least—have a footnote that gives the option "faith of Christ"? You will find "faith of Jesus Christ" or "faith of Christ" in the Greek in Romans 3:22; Galatians 2:16, 20; Ephesians 3:12; Philippians 3:9; and in other places. Many, many scholars—such as Morna Hooker, Lady Margaret professor emeritus at Cambridge University, and Michael Eaton—have defended *pistis christou* as being the subjective genitive, meaning Jesus's own faith.

I have to turn to the King James Version to help make the case for *pistis christou* being the faith *of* Jesus Christ. I am so glad the godly translators of 1611 translated it as they did, or few would ever come to see that the merit of our justification is Jesus's very faith, not merely faith in Him. Of course it means believing in Him as well. But as we will see later, Galatians 2:16 states that we believe *in* Him in order to be justified *by* the faith *of* Christ. His faith, as I said, is the meritorious cause. We believe in Him in order to have the benefit of His perfect faith. The translators of the King James Version of 1611 almost always only *translated* the Greek—literally—rather than *interpret* it. This is partly why the KJV is more difficult to read than a modern version. The trouble with so many modern versions is that whereas they do make it easier to read, they too often interpret rather than translate and sometimes paraphrase as well.

"Faith to faith," then, means Jesus's faith must be followed by our faith; His faith must be ratified by my faith. If Paul had said that in the Gospel a righteousness from

God is revealed by the faith of Christ alone, then Barth and Torrance would be right—and everybody will go to Heaven. But because Paul said a righteousness from God is revealed "from faith to faith," the only meaning that makes sense is that Christ's faith must be ratified by our faith. To show how the NIV for some reason did not want to translate the Greek "faith to faith," it paraphrases it "from first to last," which makes no sense to me.

All this becomes even clearer when we trace Paul's mind in Romans and Galatians. He uses the term "righteousness from God" first in Romans 1:17 when Paul says it is revealed "from faith to faith." He turns to the phrase "righteousness from God" in Romans 3:22 and shows exactly what he meant by "faith to faith": "Even the righteousness of God which is by faith of Jesus Christ unto all and upon all them that believe" (KJV). There it is: the faith of Jesus Christ and our faith. In other words, the faith of Christ alone does not get us to Heaven; we too need to believe. The meritorious faith of Christ needs to be joined by our faith—or there is no justification.

GALATIANS 2:16

If one needs more evidence for this, one may look at Galatians 2:16 (KJV):

> Knowing that a man is not justified by the works of the law, but by the faith of Jesus Christ, even we have believed in Jesus Christ that we might be justified by the faith of Christ, and not by the works of the law: for by the works of the law shall no flesh be justified.

This verse truly reads by itself and should need no comment. But I will call attention to the obvious: Paul says it *twice* in Galatians 2:16. The first part of the verse says we are justified "by the faith of Jesus Christ." He might have stopped there, having stated the meritorious cause for God's righteousness being imputed to us. But had he stopped there, the Barthians of this world would have seized on it! But Paul is no Barthian! So he says more in the same verse: "Even we have believed in Jesus Christ that we might be justified by the faith of Christ." In other words, being justified by the faith of Jesus is what is at the bottom of our being saved. We believe *in order* (Greek: *hina*—"in order that") that we might have claim upon the faith of Jesus Christ. I'm sorry, but it is sad to see the way modern versions translate Galatians 2:16. They always make faith in Christ redundant by rejecting the subjective genitive that is meant by *pistis christou*—saying twice if not thrice in the same verse that we believe in Christ.

The faith of Jesus Christ is Paul's term for the atoning work of our substitute. By this term Paul means:

1. Christ's life (Rom. 5:10)

2. Christ's faith (Gal. 2:20)

3. Christ's death (Rom. 5:9)

4. Christ's resurrection (Rom. 3:25)

5. Christ's intercession (as the writer of
   Hebrews says in Heb. 7:25)

Then Paul shows in Galatians 2:20 how Christians must *apply* the faith of Christ to their lives. Galatians 2:20 is one of the most magnificent, glorious, and awesome verses in the Bible. One could write a book on this verse alone. But I am dealing primarily with the Gospel and must draw the line on how much to go into it. In short, here is how the faith of Christ may be applied: "I *live* by the faith of the Son of God" (KJV, emphasis added). It is a lifestyle. The Greek is probably best translated "I live by faith [or faithfulness], namely, that of the Son of God." Paul applies Galatians 2:20 in a manner that encompasses at least three things:

1. How he knows he has been justified—he lives not by works but by Christ's life and death.

2. How Christ lives in him—and how this causes us to make a difference in the world by our lives.

3. He lives by the thrilling knowledge that Christ is praying for us at the right hand of God.

Galatians 2:20 therefore embraces Christ's priestly work at God's right hand where He ever lives to make intercession for us (Heb. 7:25). At God's right hand Jesus intercedes with a perfect faith, and we can live by it!

> This instant now I may receive
> The answer of His powerful prayer;
> This instant now by Him I live,
> His prevalence with God declare.
> —CHARLES WESLEY (1707–1788)
> "ENTERED THE HOLY PLACE ABOVE"[5]

The Meaning and
Application of Habakkuk 2:4

Paul quotes Habakkuk 2:4 two times—in Romans 1:17 and Galatians 3:11—and it is quoted again in Hebrews 10:38. The Hebrew in Habakkuk 2:4 is best translated "The righteous shall live by His [that is, God's] faithfulness." The apostle Paul would have known that well when he uses Habakkuk 2:4. One is not living by his own righteousness—hardly! We live by His! The believer leans on God's righteousness and faithfulness. This is exactly the way Hebrews 10:38 applies it. The writer had exhorted the Hebrew Christians not to give up. "For he who promised is faithful" (Heb. 10:23). That said, says the writer, we live by God's faithfulness to keep His word. And this is the way Paul applies this perspective in Galatians 2:20.

It is faith in God's faithfulness, faith in the faith of our Savior. The good news: we do not need a great faith to be saved; we need any measure of faith in a great Savior!

If Only

Some might wish that Paul had said that the justice of God is revealed "from faith to baptism." Baptism is something one might request. But that could be done without being convinced of the efficacy of Christ's blood in one's heart. I'm sorry, but baptism will not save you.

What if Paul had said "from faith to works"? That would mean we would be under obligation to perform good works without ever knowing if our works were good enough.

What if Paul had said "from faith to morality"? All that would be required of you is clean living. If only.

What if Paul had said "from faith to church membership"? That is what some seem to think saves them! Wrong. It does not take the work of the Holy Spirit to make one join a church. One may do it for social reasons!

What if Paul had said "from faith to social involvement"? There is a kind of Christianity that equates the faith with social involvement. I believe we should be socially involved. But that has nothing to do with how we get to Heaven.

What if Paul had said "from faith to being born in a Christian home"? Being born into a Christian home gives one a head start. But it does not save until the person who was born in a Christian home eventually comes to see for himself or herself the need to embrace the Gospel.

What if Paul had said "from faith to sincerity"? Sincerity is not good enough. "There is a way which seemeth right unto a man, but the end thereof are the ways of death" (Prov. 14:12, KJV).

Some may wish Paul had said "from faith to education." I'm sorry, but God is not impressed with our education.

What if Paul had said "from faith to money"? This is very like buying indulgences as they were doing in Luther's day. But God does not want your money.

But God does say:

> Come, everyone who thirsts, come to the waters;
> and he who has no money, come, buy and eat!
> Come, buy wine and milk without money and
> without price.
> —ISAIAH 55:1

Salvation is a gift, a free gift (Rom. 6:23). It is free. All you need do is to accept it. Suppose you are in Victoria station in London and are convinced that the train at gate four is going to Brighton. But it will not take *you* to Brighton unless you get on board! You accept this gift of salvation by praying this prayer:

> *Lord Jesus, I need You. I want You. I know I am a sinner. I am sorry for my sins. Wash my sins away by Your blood. I welcome Your Holy Spirit into my heart. As best as I know how I give You my life. Amen.*

Paul's doctrine of faith comes to one thing: relying on what Jesus Christ did for us—by His life and His death. When you do that you are ensured of Heaven when you die.

THREE "CAUSES" OF JUSTIFICATION

The teaching of this chapter is essential to a full understanding of the Gospel. This is because the faith of Christ is the *meritorious* cause of justification. It bestows the glory of our salvation to Jesus Christ alone. There is nothing salvific about our own faith. No man or woman can glory in his or her own faith; faith is the instrument—imparted by the Spirit—that ratifies Christ's meritorious faith. John Calvin's life overlapped Luther's somewhat, although the two men never met. Calvin's teaching and preaching came some twenty years or so after Luther's prime. Calvin therefore had time for Luther's teaching to gel. Calvin embellished—but did not contradict—Luther's teaching of justification by faith and came up with three causes of justification:

1. The meritorious cause (what Christ did for us)
2. The instrumental cause (our faith)
3. The effectual cause (the Holy Spirit's enabling power)

It is therefore not faith that saves; it is God who saves. It is Christ who saves! What Jesus Christ did is the meritorious cause of our being justified.

This is why we believe *in* Jesus Christ *in order to be justified by the faith of* Christ (Gal. 2:16). Jesus's faith is what directly led to His sinless life, keeping the Law and atoning for our sins. What is more, Paul pointed to the meritorious cause when, instead of repeating that we are justified by *faith*, he said that we are "justified by his blood" (Rom. 5:9).

JUSTIFIED BY HIS BLOOD

I invite you to ponder this for a moment: we are justified by Christ's *blood*. Does Paul contradict himself having said we are justified by faith (Rom. 5:1) and a few verses later saying we are justified by the blood of Jesus? Absolutely not. He is showing that what Jesus did for us by shedding His precious blood is what *merits* our being spared from God's terrible wrath to come; that is, assuming we rest our case in what Jesus Christ did for us. It is another way of saying faith to faith; our faith puts into effect what Jesus did by dying for us.

When Jesus ascended to the right hand of God, He sat down. The Old Testament priests always stood when doing their ministry (Heb. 10:11). But Jesus sits (Heb. 1:3). At some point after shedding His blood on the cross, He sprinkled His blood on the mercy seat in Heaven. That is where Jesus is now—in Heaven at the right hand of God. He is reigning. He is waiting for the moment He can leave His throne, but not until He makes His enemies His footstool (Ps. 110:1; 1 Cor. 15:25). While He waits for that moment, He intercedes. Does He doubt when He prays for us? Unthinkable! He intercedes with the same perfect faith He demonstrated on the earth.

No wonder, then, that can Paul say that he lives by the faith of the Son of God.

CHAPTER EIGHT

GENUINE, NOT COUNTERFEIT, FAITH

If you confess with your mouth that Jesus is Lord and believe in your heart that God raised him from the dead, you will be saved. For with the heart one believes and is justified, and with the mouth one confesses and is saved.
—ROMANS 10:9–10

WOULD YOU LIKE to sit in the chair of George Whitefield (1714–1770)?" I would often say that to people who came into the Westminster Chapel vestry. Dozens of American ministers—from Billy Graham to Arthur Blessitt—would eagerly sit in a chair that was on loan to us from the Congregational Library. Many would fancy a special "anointing" that might pass on to them. I too sat in that chair for hours over the years. George Whitefield's name and dates were embedded in a metal plate on the back of the chair. An unpretentious-looking chair, barely upholstered, it was a feature of the vestry we were proud of.

However, a couple of years before I retired, the deacons thought it would be a good idea to buy the chair from the

Congregational Library lest they ask for it back one day. We also wanted to repair it and give it new upholstery. The question was, Would it hurt the value of the chair if we reupholstered it? So I wrote to Sotheby's of London, the undoubted world experts on antiques. They examined it and later replied, first, "It's not Whitefield's chair; this chair is clearly in the period 1840–1850"; second, "It will not hurt its value if you reupholster it."

Oh dear. Our balloon suddenly burst. We immediately returned the chair to the Congregational Library. I have thought a lot about the pride and joy of having George Whitefield's chair all those years. This led me to think of the word of the Lord to Jeremiah: "I have made you a tester of metals among my people.... Rejected silver they are called, for the LORD has rejected them" (Jer. 6:27, 30). In other words, they were counterfeit silver, not true silver.

It is not always easy to recognize the counterfeit. I have probably handled counterfeit money many times without knowing it. I bought a gold watch in Rome for forty dollars, telling Louise I got a good deal. "It really is worth hundreds," I said to her. (She was not happy I bought the watch from this kid on the streets.) But when I tried to sell it in Switzerland to an authentic jeweler, he said it is not worth one dollar! I was hoodwinked. I was climbing on the Temple Mount in Jerusalem. Two Arab boys showed me a coin they claimed they had just found and offered it to me for a hundred dollars. It looked like an ancient Roman coin. I took all the money I had on me—about fifty dollars—and gave it to them. I noticed they ran like mad! I found out why when I took it to a gold dealer in Jerusalem; it was a fake, not worth a penny!

So we had a counterfeit Whitefield chair in the vestry all those years. The chair looked credible to all of us; it also gave many a visitor a lot of pleasure. People took photographs of it and photographs of themselves sitting in the chair and standing beside it. But the Whitefield chair was false. Phony. Fake. Counterfeit.

Church leaders too can be counterfeit. Preachers can be counterfeit. Prophets can be counterfeit. The apostle Paul spoke of men who masquerade as apostles of Christ: "...and no wonder, for even Satan disguises himself as an angel of light. So it is no surprise if his servants, also, disguise themselves as servants of righteousness" (2 Cor. 11:13–15).

COUNTERFEIT FAITH

So too can people making professions of faith appear at first to be pure gold when they are actually "fool's gold." A lot of people in the 1850s in the Old West in America presumed themselves wealthy overnight when they thought they had discovered gold in streams of water. Sometimes this turned out to be iron sulfide, which had a metallic luster and a pale brass-yellow hue; it gave a superficial appearance of gold. It became known as fool's gold.

On my first trip to Israel there was a winsome Arab man—Omar—who stood just outside our Jerusalem hotel. He sold beads and souvenirs. He would say to us as we walked to our bus, "Want to buy some beads? Buy some beads! Jesus saves! Jesus is coming soon. I make special price for you. Jesus saves!" People on our bus—including me—bought a lot of stuff from him. On the last Sunday we all went to the eleven o'clock service at the Southern Baptist Church in East Jerusalem. Lo and behold, Omar came to church and sat on the back row. People were pleased to see him. My friend Dr. Jess Moody preached the sermon and then gave an invitation for anyone present to receive Christ. One person came forward—Omar! Everyone was thrilled. Jess Moody wept. That is, until we left the building to find that Omar got outside first, shouting, "Beads. Beads. Want to buy some beads. Jesus is coming soon! Jesus saves! Better buy some beads." Dear Jess shook his head and tried to smile. Some thought Omar was saved. But Jess realized Omar was a shrewd businessman!

WHAT THE COUNTERFEIT CAN PRODUCE

Saving faith—not walking forward in an evangelistic rally—is what gets you to Heaven. Not all who walk forward turn out to have a counterfeit faith. Not all who have saving faith walk forward. It is only belief in the *heart* wherever you are—as long as the Lord Jesus Christ is the object of that faith—that is saving faith. One can ask for baptism out of a counterfeit faith. One can join a church and have counterfeit faith. One can manifest certain fruits of piety without being truly saved. One can have the gift of prophecy and be unsaved. One can have the gift of miracles and cast out devils and be lost. Jesus said:

> On that day many will say to me, "Lord, Lord, did we not prophesy in your name, and cast out demons in your name, and do many mighty

works in your name?" And then will I declare to them, "I never knew you; depart from me, you workers of lawlessness."

—MATTHEW 7:22–23

I offered three valid definitions of *saving faith*. Saving faith is relying on the truth of the Gospel. It is believing in your heart that He died for you. It is trusting His blood, not your works. It is believing in your heart that Jesus is God, that He is the God-man. In a word, it is relying on Christ. You can only do this if you *believe in your heart* that Jesus is God and that He was raised from the dead. The key: when you believe these things in your heart.

Only *you* know if you believe these things in your heart. If you have to *ask*, "Do I believe this in my heart?" you don't. You know if you do. You know if you don't.

FAITH IS ASSURANCE

The root word for the Greek *pistis*—faith—is *peitho*, which means "persuasion."[1] This is very, very important. Being persuaded—being assured—is an essential ingredient of true faith. It is not head knowledge; it touches the heart. It is not mental assent to certain teachings. It is not showing emotion. It is not shedding tears. Or even making strides in keeping the Law.

> Not the labor of my hands
> Can fulfill Thy law's demands;
> Could my zeal no respite know,
> Could my tears forever flow,

All for sin could not atone,
Thou must save, and Thou alone.
—Augustus Toplady (1740–1778)
Rock of Ages[2]

You must answer the questions "What do I *really* believe to be true? Is my faith based upon secondhand information?" It is like what the Queen of Sheba said to King Solomon. She had heard about his achievements and wisdom. She heard this in her own country—many miles away. "But I did not *believe* the report until I came and my own eyes had seen it" (1 Kings 10:7, emphasis added). This is what persuaded her. She believed when she saw for herself and was persuaded.

However, faith to be *faith* is being persuaded by evidence of things *not seen*. "Now faith is the assurance of things hoped for, the conviction of things not seen" (Heb. 11:1). The Queen of Sheba believed because she *saw*. But you cannot call this *faith*. Thomas believed that Jesus was raised from the dead because he saw the risen, physical person of Jesus before his eyes. So Jesus said to him, "Blessed are those who have not seen and yet have believed" (John 20:29). Faith is believing without seeing.

The secular atheist only believes what he or she senses—what is seen, felt, smelled, tasted, or heard with the physical body. The Jews shouted at Jesus on the cross, "Come down now from the cross that we may *see and believe*" (Mark 15:32, emphasis added). That is the order that the *natural man* (or woman) requires. "I will believe it when I see it." But if one sees first and then believes, you can no longer call this *faith*. What the Queen of Sheba saw was not by faith. What Thomas saw was not by faith. It is only faith when you cannot see—but still believe. "So faith comes from hearing, and hearing through the word of Christ" (Rom. 10:17). Such "hearing" is not by our physical ears, although we do need to hear the message through our physical ears. Hearing the message with our physical ears is the point of entry. One cannot hear unless the Gospel has been shared first. But the hearing Paul speaks of is an *inner hearing*. It is an inner persuasion that comes by the Holy Spirit. John Calvin called it the "internal testimony of the Holy Spirit." He defined *faith* as "a firm and certain knowledge of God's benevolence toward us, founded on the truth of the freely given promise in Christ, both revealed to our minds, and sealed upon our hearts, through the Holy Spirit."[3]

The Holy Spirit imparts the persuasion. He instills the faith. Faith is the gift of God (Eph. 2:8). The persuasion, though you do not see with your physical eyes, is so powerful you would stake your life on it—said Martin Luther—a "thousand times." Luther defined *faith* as "a living, bold trust in God's grace, so certain of God's favor that it would risk death a thousand times trusting in it."[4]

It is assurance without good works. If you are required to show works to convince yourself you have faith, you will base your assurance on works every time. But the faith of the Gospel is assurance without works. You get your assurance by looking to Christ. "There is life in a look," said Charles Spurgeon. He exhorted, "Run to the cross. If you can't run, walk. If you can't walk, crawl. If you can't crawl, look."

There are those who assert justification by faith but

assurance by works. This is bad theology. For if faith is a persuasion, it means you are already assured. There is assurance in faith. Where there is no assurance, one looks to works. That would mean looking to yourself—not Christ. Yet Theodore Beza (1519–1605), John Calvin's successor in Geneva, sadly argued that making your calling and election sure means beginning with yourself, "descending into ourselves"—the opposite of what Calvin taught. Calvin said, "If you contemplate yourself, that is sure damnation."[5] The English Puritans followed Beza, not Calvin, and the outlook for the Puritans and their hearers was introspection, legalism, and gloom. Whatever happened to the Gospel? It gave way to gloom, doom, legalism, and introspection.

THE PRIESTHOOD
OF THE BELIEVER

One of the lesser emphasized but very important fruits of the Great Reformation is the rediscovery of the priesthood of the believer. Instead of needing a priest to confess to, you may confess to God directly without a priest. You don't need someone else to tell you that you are forgiven; you know you are forgiven because you believe in your heart. If you need a priest or preacher to tell you how you know you have saving faith, it is probably because you have not been convinced in your heart yet. But if you believe in your heart that Jesus is God, that is enough! If you believe in your heart that God forgives you because of what Christ has done, that is enough! If you believe in your heart that God raised Jesus from the dead, that is enough! We do not need good works to bolster your faith when saving faith is seated in the heart—not the intellect, not our emotions, not your zeal. Saving faith is not based on anything you have done. It is relying on Jesus Christ directly. Not indirectly by beginning with your works, but directly without anything else!

For any minister or priest not to grant you the privilege of being your own priest, running roughshod over what you as a person believe, is thrusting an indignity on you. It is encouraging you to trust only another person's opinion for approval.

When people ignore your right and privilege to believe the Gospel in your heart by superimposing their opinion that you must *prove* this by good works, they violate your dignity and integrity. They remove your right to think for yourself. They rob you of the privilege of knowing that you know. They also go beyond Scripture.

CHAPTER NINE

FAITH AND WORKS

*You have dishonored the poor
man.... Can that faith save him?*
—JAMES 2:6, 14

MARTIN LUTHER WASN'T perfect. He had at least two major blind spots. First, which is very sad, he did not esteem Jews and said horrible things about them. I am sorry about this and am also ashamed of him whenever I think of this. He based his comments on the fact that the Jews rejected Jesus Christ as their Messiah. Luther's position is utterly wrong and is no basis for hating Jews or anyone else who rejects the Gospel.

Not only that; Luther seems to have overlooked that at the beginning of the Book of Romans—a book that he loved—Paul said that the Gospel was *still* offered to the Jew "first" and then to the Gentile (Rom. 1:16). This also means that Jews need to be saved, that is, converted by the Spirit of God, and affirm Jesus of Nazareth as their true Messiah, or they will be eternally lost. Away with the notion that Jews get a second chance! This teaching is misleading and dangerous. When I wrote my book with Rabbi Sir David

Rosen, *The Christian and the Pharisee* (his choice for a title), he said to me, "According to you Christians, we Jews get a second chance."[1] I shot back, "No," to him. But that erroneous idea had reached him, giving him and all Jews a feeling that they don't need to believe the Gospel when they hear it. They will be given a second chance. So wrong. So horrible that anyone would say this. The Jews—every one of them—certainly do need to embrace the Gospel of Jesus Christ, or they too will be eternally lost—as any Gentile would be.

A few years ago David and Sharon Rosen invited us into their home for a memorable Shabbat meal one Friday evening. During our conversation I casually referred to Martin Luther, affirming his contribution to church history. David's daughter was present for the meal, and she was visibly shocked and horrified that I would say something good about Luther. But David knew what I was doing and explained to his daughter that I was referring to Luther's teaching of justification by faith. But it taught me a lesson: it is very unwise indeed to mention Martin Luther to a Jew in a complimentary way.

Martin Luther's second blind spot was his failure to understand the Book of James. He saw it as "an epistle of straw" and sadly asserted, even a year before his death, "We will not teach that book here." Luther saw James's teaching regarding faith and works as a threat because he thought—wrongly—that it contradicted his own teaching on justification by faith alone.

I must be fair. I have condemned the ancient heretic Marcion and the modern-day hyper-grace people for their rejecting books in the New Testament that did not sit well with their teaching. But Luther was, in effect, no different; he rejected the Book of James.

Martin Luther had totally dedicated his life, ministry, and reputation to his understanding of justification by *faith without works*. It had become almost personal with him. He became hypersensitive about this issue. So James includes a verse that apparently categorically contradicts Luther's teaching. It is the famous James 2:14 of this wonderful epistle.

JAMES 2:14

> What good is it, my brothers, if someone says he has faith but does not have works? Can that faith save him?

The obvious answer to James's question is *no*. The answer is *no* if the verse stands alone; it is *no* if the verse is understood in its context.

That said, there is a *huge* difference in understanding James 2:14 *in* its context and when it stands alone *outside* its context. I admit that the natural reading of James 2:14 can lead one to believe that James is talking about assurance of salvation. But that is only when it is read *outside its context*. The problem is, it seems, that everyone—including Luther—read James 2:14 as if it stands alone outside its context. People therefore invariably seem to assume it refers to whether a person has saving faith. They assume James is saying that whoever claims to have faith without works is not saved. "Can faith save him?" No.

Therefore when James 2:14 stands alone outside its

context, it would appear to refer to whether or not the person himself who makes the claim "I have faith" is saved.

I had never been convinced that James is saying that the person of James 2:14 is not saved. A person certainly is saved by faith without works. The traditional explanation is that James is only explaining that true faith will always have works to prove its genuineness. That is the way out of this dilemma for many interpreters. Or take the cliché: "We are justified by faith alone, but justifying faith is never alone." Oh, how this misses the point!

That is not what James is saying at all. For faith without works does save that person! That is the whole argument of Paul in Galatians and Romans.

But aren't we urged to have works to demonstrate that we have faith? Yes. But James does not say that to prove anything to *ourselves.* The greatest freedom is having nothing to prove. If we are already persuaded, we don't need works to prove to ourselves what is genuine. I know whether or not I am relying on Christ for my salvation; I don't need works to prove to myself that I am saved!

However, the world out there does not know that. They cannot read our minds. They can't examine our hearts. They only know what they *see* in us. Therefore we need to demonstrate our good works to reach *others.* Jesus taught that we should let our light shine before people that they may see our good works and glorify our Father in Heaven (Matt. 5:16). We demonstrate good works, then, 1) in order to obey our Lord and glorify our heavenly Father; and 2) to demonstrate that we really do care about our witness to the world. *They* need to see something in us that will make them want to have what we have.

As I said, Martin Luther disliked the Book of James because *his* reading of it contradicted Paul's teaching of justification by faith. This is because he did not interpret James 2:14 in the context of the preceding verses of that chapter. Luther was *so* wrong. There is no contradiction at all. If only he knew that James was his very dear friend!

First, Luther needed to realize that the reference to the "poor man" in James 2:6 was the *main focus of James 2, and especially of James 2:14.* Most scholars miss this. The Greek word *ptochon* means the "poor man" (accusative, masculine, singular). The way some versions translate *ptochon* as "the poor" sounds as if it is plural, meaning many poor people. When it is read that way, you are thrown off—and unlikely to get back to James's point. Fortunately, the ESV got it right: "You have dishonored the poor man." Keep the "poor man" in mind from then on, and you are set to understand James 2:14.

Most people think James has changed the subject from the poor man to one's assurance of salvation by the time he gets to James 2:14. Wrong. He is *still* concerned about the poor man who will never be reached for the Gospel because early Jewish Christians had become social climbers. He begins in James 2:1: "My brothers, show no partiality as you hold the faith in our Lord Jesus Christ, the Lord of glory." He then paints a picture: A wealthy man comes to their meetings and is given special treatment. But the poor man wearing shabby clothes is treated with no dignity at all. James rebukes these Jewish believers for being like that; after all, God has chosen the poor to be rich in faith and to inherit the kingdom (James 2:1–5). Then he attacks the Jewish believers big time: you have dishonored the *poor man*. He chooses to use "the poor man" as an illustration of how Christian Jews treated such a person. James has the poor man in mind *throughout the entire second chapter of James*. I encourage you to read James 2 with the poor man in mind, and it will not only make complete sense to you; you will see that James does not differ from Paul one iota.

There is absolutely no contradiction to what James says and what the apostle Paul teaches in Romans and Galatians.

As I put it at the very beginning of this chapter, read it this way: "You have dishonored the poor man...can faith save him?" (NIV says "insulted"). Consider verses James 2:6–13 as if they were a parenthesis. James is saying this: "You have insulted the poor man; can faith save him?" *You dishonored the poor man; can faith save the poor man?* No. Of course not. By "save" James means win over, convince, or convert. Can faith alone win over the poor man? No. Can faith without works have an effect on the poor man? No. Can faith only have influence on the poor man? No. Can faith in and of itself convince the poor man? No. Can mere faith convert the poor man? No.

But faith *combined* with works can convince him! The poor man is not the slightest bit interested in whether we are sound in our Christology or doctrine of the Trinity. If we say that we believe there is one God—or that God is one, good. But so does the devil (James 2:19).

The mistake therefore that nearly everyone seems to make is to assume that James has changed the subject from concern for the poor to a believer's assurance of salvation. Not so. You are not even close to grasping James

2:14 if you think that. Luther was not close to what James meant. Personal assurance of salvation of the man who has faith but not works is not remotely on James's mind. He is thinking of the reputation, testimony, and influence of Jewish believers who have been unkind to that poor man out there.

James is also showing how disgusting it is to claim to have faith—and also to be sound theologically—and show contempt for the poor man. The "him" of James 2:14, never forget, is in the accusative, singular, masculine as in James 2:6. So "poor man" and "him" in James 2:14 are bound together by the Greek. It is surprising that Luther missed this when he translated the Greek into German.

Please bear with me if I relate a little journey of how I came to see this. In the summer of 1979 I felt strongly led to preach through James. But no, I thought, I am not going to begin preaching through James until I understand James 2:14—a verse that had plagued me for years. I never had peace about the traditional way of handling this, namely, that "James is only saying that true faith will inevitably be accompanied by good works." I knew in my heart of hearts that is certainly not what James says; it is what many want him to say. But whatever does it mean? I needed to know the meaning of James 2:14, or I would not proceed. But I then felt equally led to start at James 1:1. I was assured that when I get to James 2:14 I would know its meaning. The problem was when I finished James 2:13 (all these sermons are printed in the *Westminster Record*), I did not have a clue what James 2:14 meant. But on the Monday morning before the following Sunday when I would preach on this, the breakthrough came. I somehow saw that the "him" in James 2:14 was not referring to whether a person had saving faith himself but to his testimony to the unsaved poor man—"him." I discovered that the "him" of James 2:14 was accusative, masculine, singular, as in James 2:6—which no translation I was using at the time made clear. But once I saw how James 2:6 and James 2:14 were inseparably tied to each other, I knew I had gotten it right for sure.

There is one more thing some readers may find interesting. That breakthrough came during the days I spent Thursdays with Dr. Martyn Lloyd-Jones in order to go over my sermons for the following weekend. I shared this view of James 2:14 with Dr. Lloyd-Jones. I remember it as though it were yesterday; he looked at me and said, "You have convinced me"—which of course I found very encouraging. Sometime later the late Dr. and Mrs. W. A. Criswell had a meal with us when we lived in Ealing. He was equally gripped by my new insight. Michael Eaton wrote some time later—having heard my taped sermon— to say that my interpretation of James 2:14–15 not only convinced him but affected his ministry in Nairobi and led him to open his church in Johannesburg (where he was pastor at that time) to the black people of South Africa.

Therefore should Christians demonstrate works to show that they have genuine faith? Yes. Of course. But it is for the benefit of the world out there, not because you and I need a prop to our faith! John Calvin's interpretation of 2 Peter 1:10, "Confirm your calling and election," was much the same; it is to give *proof* of our faith, not for ourselves but for the world to see. In the same way, James has the non-Christian in mind but chooses the poor man as an example of how believers will never reach the poor man as long as they are aiming for the rich! Aim for the rich man, James says, and you will never reach him; aim for the poor man, and you will reach both.

One final point about the remainder of James 2:15–26. The Greek word translated "justified" in James 2:24 is better translated "vindicated," as in 1 Timothy 3:16. This completely clarifies the remaining verses in James 2, as my book *Justification by Works* shows.[2]

Do you expect to see Martin Luther in Heaven—a man who questioned whether the letter of James should be in the canon of Scripture? Do you expect to see William Perkins in Heaven, a man who went to his grave without assurance that he was a child of God? Do you expect to see those Puritans in Heaven who said you must not claim to have assurance of salvation unless good works preceded it? Do you expect to see Nazarenes in Heaven, who, speaking generally, believed they make it there by being "saved and sanctified"? Do you expect to see Mother Teresa in Heaven? Do you think that some or many Catholics will be in Heaven? Do you expect to see Pope John Paul II in Heaven?

> Therefore do not pronounce judgment before the time, before the Lord comes, who will bring to light the things now hidden in darkness and will disclose the purposes of the heart. Then each one will receive his commendation from God.
>
> —1 Corinthians 4:5

IMPLICIT FAITH

One of the least known but most important teachings of Calvin is what he calls "implicit faith." It is faith that lacks a full knowledge of truth but that is nonetheless true faith. He cited the woman of Samaria as an example. She believed what she saw and heard in Jesus. Her testimony led to many coming to confess that Jesus was "the Savior of the world" (John 4:42). But Jesus had not yet died on the cross, neither is it likely they saw Him as the God-man. But they believed what they saw. This is implicit faith, a measure of knowledge that needs to be topped up at some stage. Yet Calvin also added that there is a sense in which all faith is implicit faith. We are still learning. We have so much more to learn.

One of our members at Westminster Chapel was a young lady who was saved in a church in York. She was a student there, who went to an Anglican church where she was converted. But she had no idea there is a Hell, and her knowledge of the Gospel was quite shallow when she first came to us. She grew by leaps and bounds. But this did not mean she became a Christian after she came to us. She was truly converted in York. She no doubt had implicit faith—a genuine faith, a saving faith, but a faith that was greatly lacking in knowledge.

How right (I suspect) Luther was! The surprises we will have in Heaven. But what about those who *we were so sure* would be there but are not? Could this be some of those who seemed to be so godly? Could it be some of those who gave to the poor and put people through university? Could it be those who were faithful tithers and were faithful in church every Sunday? I think of millions—millions—of Southern Baptists, Methodists, Presbyterians, Anglicans, and Lutherans who were baptized. Some stopped coming to church a week or two after they made a profession. Some persevered. I think of thousands who went into the ministry. Seminary professors. Missionaries. Who knows?

One of my favorite professors at seminary was brought up in a solid evangelical church. He memorized scripture as a boy. He was full of zeal for the Lord. But after he got theological training, he forgot his sound background and taught the opposite of what he grew up believing. Will he be in Heaven? I think of people in my old church who would sing and shout (literally) in church. They would walk up and down the aisles of the church with tears running down their faces, waving handkerchiefs in the air—they were so full of joy. Will all of them be in Heaven? I think of preachers who were sound, orthodox, and knowledgeable—but lived in adultery while in the ministry. I think of a thoroughly Reformed pastor who left his wife and children to live a gay lifestyle. Will he be in Heaven? I think of the man who befriended me when I needed financial help many years ago—he was "saved" one week, lost the next. Will he be in Heaven? You tell me.

CHAPTER TEN

WHY BE A CHRISTIAN?

For the wrath of God is revealed from heaven against
all ungodliness and unrighteousness of men, who
by their unrighteousness suppress the truth.
—ROMANS 1:18

Therefore, knowing the fear of the Lord, we persuade others.
—2 CORINTHIANS 5:11

I N RECENT YEARS Louise and I have made four trips to Enfield, Connecticut. Often when I am either in Connecticut or Massachusetts, I make it a priority to go to Enfield, even though it has taken two hours one way to get there. In a vacant lot across the street from the Montessori school there is to be found a plaque amidst some green shrubbery, which shows that someone is looking after it. The plaque commemorates the site and message of Jonathan Edwards's notable sermon "Sinners in the Hands of an Angry God," preached on July 8, 1741, at the height of the Great Awakening.[1]

I go there to pray. I usually don't stay long. But I always ask the Lord, "Please do it again." I try to imagine what it must have been like. The old meetinghouse is gone; there remains only a vacant lot. Jonathan Edwards took his text from Deuteronomy 32:35 (KJV): "Their foot shall slide in due time." He read his sermon; it pertained to eternal punishment in Hell. The sermon summed up: *It is by the mercy of God that you are not in Hell right now. You are hanging over Hell by a slender thread, and the death angel is ready to sever that thread.*

Many people laugh at this sermon today. No one was laughing then. The power of the Spirit was so intense that people began holding on to church pews to keep from sliding into Hell. After the service people were seen holding on to tree trunks to keep from sliding into Hell. News of the sermon spread all over New England in days and spread across the Atlantic to England in weeks. It is still remembered. I gather that some citizens of Enfield are embarrassed by this site. Some ministers, theologians, and scholars today likewise do not see this event as something to be proud of. But Edwards's immortal sermon is a matter of history. The irony is Edwards preached the same sermon a few weeks later at his own church in Northampton, Massachusetts. It apparently had no effect at all. God only did it once.

The preaching of John the Baptist, "You brood of vipers! Who warned you to flee from the wrath to come?" (Matt. 3:7), made a similar impact. You may say the declaration of the coming wrath of God is the first message of the New Testament.

John the Baptist set the stage for Jesus's preaching. Not far away from those who heard or knew about the message of John the Baptist was the thought of the coming wrath of God. When Jesus said, "On that day many will say to me, 'Lord, Lord, did we not prophesy in your name, and cast out demons in your name, and do many mighty works in your name?'" (Matt. 7:22), He did not need to explain what "that day" is. All knew. The Old Testament prophets had forecast "the day of the Lord" (e.g., Isa. 2:12; Joel 2:31). On the Day of Pentecost, Peter's sermon quoted Joel: "The sun shall be turned to darkness and the moon to blood, before the day of the Lord comes, the great and magnificent day" (Acts 2:20). The response was that the hearers were "cut to the heart" and asked, "What shall we do?" (Acts 2:37). All were filled with fear (Acts 2:43, KJV).

I am not against "seeker-friendly" churches as long as they preach the Gospel to those who are present. I don't mean to be unfair, but I am not sure how the preaching of Hell and eternal punishment fits into a seeker-friendly atmosphere.

Why do you suppose people should be Christians? Do you believe all people should be Christians? If so, why? Do you believe your loved ones should be Christians? Do you want your children to be Christians? Why? Do you believe your neighbors should be Christians? Do you believe the people you work with—whether your boss or those near you—should become Christians? In a word, do you believe that *all* men and women should be Christians? Why?

The Book of Romans is addressed "to all those in Rome who are loved by God" (Rom. 1:7). Romans is not written strictly for the non-Christian; it is written to those "who are called to belong to Jesus Christ" (Rom. 1:6). That said, any non-Christian may well read Romans and be converted. I certainly hope any non-Christian could read my own book and be converted. If that person should be *you*, I can assure you that I have prayed for you. It is my supreme wish that you will come to Christ in faith as a direct result from reading this book. Nothing would thrill me more than for this to happen.

As we saw above, Paul wastes no time in getting to the heart of his letter to the Romans. He states that he is unashamed of the Gospel because it is the power of God for *salvation* (Rom. 1:16). He introduces his doctrine of justification by faith (Rom. 1:17) and then plunges into the *reason* people need to be saved:

> For [Greek: *gar*, or "because"] the wrath of God is revealed from heaven against all ungodliness and unrighteousness of men, who by their unrighteousness suppress the truth.
> —ROMANS 1:18

Why should people be Christians? In a word, because of *the wrath of God*. That's it. This is why people need salvation. There is a Hell.

Of course there are other reasons. But the primary reason according to John the Baptist, Jesus, and the apostle Paul is because people will "perish" if they do not believe in Christ (John 3:16).

Some people say: "I believe in Heaven, but I don't believe in Hell."

I reply: "If there is no Hell, there is no Heaven." The same Bible teaches both and, if anything, says more about Hell than it does about Heaven.

People need to be saved so that they will go to Heaven and not to Hell.

Do you believe this?

We all have probably heard people say, "If there were no Heaven and no Hell, I would still be a Christian." I heard that when I was a boy in my old church in Kentucky. Why would people say that? With good reason! They have found that having God as your Father and Holy Spirit as your guide *can* make life so sweet and wonderful. What would we do without prayer? What would we do without the Bible? What would we do without God's guidance? The God of the Bible—the God who saves us—gives us the Holy Spirit for a close walk with God. The God of the Bible supplies our need (Phil. 4:19); He gives us our jobs, our homes, our possessions, our friends. He delivers us in a time of trouble. He paves the way for us when we are not even thinking about Him. He makes things happen on our behalf. He steps in when we need Him most—never too late, never too early, but always just in time.

I could so easily get diverted at this precise moment to testify of God's goodness—how He led me to Trevecca; to my being called to preach; to my first church; to my wife, Louise; to our children; to supplying our need to get to England; to Westminster Chapel; to a ministry in my old age that takes me right around the world. The astonishing providence of God alone is enough to convince us that *everybody should be a Christian!*

But that is not the reason Paul gives. Not at all. Does this surprise you? Instead of being seeker friendly, Paul picks up the strain of the Old Testament prophets, of John the Baptist, and of Jesus, who warn of what is coming down the road. The reason people need to be justified— made just, or righteous—is because of the justice of God.

The righteousness of God. The holiness of God. The jealousy of God. The wrath of God. And, thankfully, the mercy, kindness, and love of God.

This may not sound as if Paul is wanting to make it easy for you to want to become a Christian. Yet this is the same Paul who says:

> For though I am free from all, I have made myself a servant to all, that I might win more of them. To the Jews I became as a Jew, in order to win Jews. To those under the law I became as one under the law (though not being myself under the law), that I might win those under the law....To the weak I became weak, that I might win the weak. I have become all things to all people, that by all means I might save some. I do it all for the sake of the gospel, that I may share with them in its blessings.
> —1 CORINTHIANS 9:19–23

Do these words to the Corinthians contradict what Paul says in Romans about the coming wrath of God?

Not at all. It is *because* of the coming wrath of God that Paul is prepared to go out of his way and make sacrifices in order to win all he can to Jesus Christ. He is prepared to be seeker friendly, yes; but he will never, never, never sweep the offense of the cross or the teaching of the wrath of God under the carpet to get more people to sign up.

Billy Graham's latest book—*Where I Am: Heaven, Eternity, and Our Life Beyond*—is a book I recommend to you.[2] I was given a copy when I preached at The Cove (the Billy Graham Training Center) last year. A good portion of this book deals with the subject of Hell and pulls no punches. As Billy awaits his call to glory, he leaves behind this book that lets us all know exactly what he believes about Heaven and Hell.

What do you suppose Paul would say to you if he heard you say, "If there were no Heaven and no Hell, I would still be a Christian"? I can safely tell you what he would say, "Not me." Paul not only would reply, "I would not say that," but would state categorically, "If in Christ we have hope in this life only, we are of all people most to be pitied" (1 Cor. 15:19).

INCALCULABLE BENEFITS

There are incalculable fringe benefits of being a Christian—prayer; intimacy with the Holy Spirit; guidance; material blessings; reading the Bible; God's extraordinary providence; finding your true friends; witnessing Him opening doors and closing the wrong doors; God showing up never too late, never too early, but always just on time; healing; the gifts and fruits of the Spirit; manifesting His love when we least deserve it; and countless other things. But the mistake some people make is making the fringe benefits of being a Christian the main reason to become a Christian.

There are some who testify, "My marriage was saved by my becoming a Christian." I believe this. And many have written to me to say that my book *Total Forgiveness* either saved their marriage or transformed it.[3] But some statistics suggest otherwise—that the number of marriages ending in divorce where the marriage ceremony took place in a church are much the same as when the ceremony took place outside the church. Some testify, "I've never been so happy in my life as I am since I became a Christian." I believe them.

One of the people who came to Christ at my former church in Fort Lauderdale, Florida, and whom I baptized, was standing outside the church one Sunday evening, looking at the stars. He was weeping. I said, "Are you all right, George?"

"Yes, I'm fine. I am just asking why it took me so long to believe." He seemed so happy.

But not everybody would say this. The first person I baptized at Westminster Chapel was Jay Michaels. He was a Jew—a Los Angeles businessman who had an office in London. His secretary invited him to come and hear me preach. He was converted the same night. I found this out months later. We became friends. I took him bonefishing in the Florida Keys. He gave Louise and me tickets for Centre Court at Wimbledon. He became like family. Yet one day he said to me, "Before I was a Christian, I was a happy man." He wasn't joking, and he wasn't complaining. He was simply reporting that it had been far from easy for him since he was converted. The sermon he heard me preach on the night of his conversion was on Heaven—where he is today—and being ready to go to Heaven when you die.

I don't blame any minister, pastor, evangelist, or soul winner who uses all sorts of means to entice people to come to Christ—whether it is the testimony of a rock singer, an actress, a musician, or businessman. As Jesus healed people in more than one way, so there are many ways to motivate people to come to Christ. If Jonathan Edwards's sermon was the only way to get people saved, why did not the Holy Spirit own the same sermon weeks later when he preached it in Northampton? I am not recommending that every evangelist or minister should preach on Hell and eternal punishment every time one speaks.

HOW PAUL'S LIFE CHANGED AFTER HE WAS SAVED

Although I am certainly not against people giving their testimonies at evangelistic rallies, telling why they became Christians and how their lives have changed, I wonder how many of us in the ministry would dare show how Paul's life changed after his conversion. We know he was struck to the ground by the Holy Spirit. He was blind for three days and was then healed. He was granted repentance—making a one-hundred-eighty degree turn in his life. He immediately began teaching that Jesus Christ was the Son of God. Whereas before conversion he was the number one persecutor of Christians, he was suddenly put on the most wanted list by Jews after that. He had been told that he would suffer for the Lord (Acts 9:16).

Have you ever examined how much Paul suffered? So how would the testimonies below do in an evangelistic rally? Listen to him now. Tell us, Paul, how has it been since you became a Christian? He answers in a manner that you might put the following as the contents for his talk: "What Christianity has done for me."

> We have become a spectacle to the world, to angels, and to men. We are fools for Christ's sake....To the present hour we hunger and thirst,

we are poorly dressed and buffeted and homeless,
and we labor, working with our own hands. . . . We
have become, and are still, like the scum of the
world, the refuse of all things.

—1 CORINTHIANS 4:9–13

And unless you think that was a one-off predicament for
Paul—then written around AD 55, listen to him some two
years later. Things did not get better for him. He wasn't
enjoying five-star hotels or riding in his own private jet. If
anything, things went from bad to worse!

Five times I received at the hands of the Jews the
forty lashes less one. Three times I was beaten
with rods. Once I was stoned. Three times I was
shipwrecked; a night and a day I was adrift at
sea; on frequent journeys, in danger from rivers,
danger from robbers, danger from my own
people, danger from Gentiles, danger in the city,
danger in the wilderness, danger at sea, danger
from false brothers; in toil and hardship, through
many a sleepless night, in hunger and thirst, often
without food, in cold and exposure.

—2 CORINTHIANS 11:24–27

Do you think that would persuade many to become a
Christian?

Why be a Christian? Paul's reply: because of the wrath
of God that is coming.

Why be a Christian? Because eternity lasts a long time.

Why be a Christian? Because Christianity is not all
about this life.

CHAPTER ELEVEN

HELL

In Hades, being in torment, he lifted up his eyes and saw Abraham far off and Lazarus at his side. And he called out, "Father Abraham, have mercy on me, and send Lazarus to dip the end of his finger in water and cool my tongue, for I am in anguish in this flame."
—LUKE 16:23–24

I N HIS ADDRESS to the first graduating class of The Salvation Army, William Booth (1878–1912) began his talk like this: "Brothers and sisters, perhaps I should apologize to you for keeping you here for two years—all so that you could learn how to lead a lost soul to Jesus Christ. It would have been better had you spent five minutes in hell."[1] The implication of this latter line was you would not need to be taught; you would be so stirred and convinced of the awfulness of Hell and people's need to be saved that you would speak to the lost everywhere, warning of the wrath to come and therefore would surely lead many to Christ.

Why be a Christian? I repeat: because eternity lasts a long time. All people in the world who ever lived will be alive and well in one of two final destinies: Heaven or Hell. This is why Jesus asked the unanswerable question: What does it profit a man or woman to gain the *whole world*—unlikely—but lose *his or her own soul*? (Mark 8:36). What will your millions be worth when you die? What will your popularity be worth one hundred years from now? One thousand years from now? One million years from now?

I think of the final verse of John Newton's hymn "Amazing Grace":

> When we've been there ten thousand years
> Bright shining as the sun,
> We've no less days to sing God's praise
> Than when we'd first begun.
> —John Newton (1725–1807)[2]

Put that sublime line in reverse, and consider someone in Hell ten thousand years from now. It is impossible to fathom how fearful, awful, and terrible this is.

This brings the question "Why be a Christian?" into the most sobering perspective I can imagine. Remember, if there is no Hell, there is no Heaven. If there is no everlasting Hell, there is no everlasting Heaven. You have no right to believe in Heaven (because it is so pleasant) except that the Bible teaches it. And the same Bible gives even more space to the subject of the lost in Hell than it does to joy in Heaven.

Jesus's words put it simply, succinctly, and clearly: "And these will go away into eternal punishment, but the righteous into eternal life" (Matt. 25:46). If you ask any unbiased person who had nothing to prove to read this verse, what do you suppose he would think it means? The natural reading is obvious: eternal punishment lasts as long as eternal life.

C. S. Lewis said, "I have met no people who fully disbelieved in hell and also had a living and life-giving belief in Heaven. The biblical teaching on both destinations stands or falls together. When heaven and hell are spoken of in Scripture, each place is portrayed as being just as real and, in some passages anyway, as permanent as the other."[3]

Jesus's words: "And these will go away into eternal punishment, but the righteous into eternal life" (Matt. 25:46). Or with the words of Revelation 20:10, which speaks of not only Satan but two human beings, the Antichrist and the false prophet, being cast into the lake of fire and "tormented day and night forever and ever." Revelation 14:11 appears to apply to a large number of people: "And the smoke of their torment goes up forever and ever."

In the Bible, Jesus spoke more about Hell than anyone else did. He referred to Hell as a real place (Matt. 10:28; 13:40–42; Mark 9:43–48). He described it in graphic terms: a fire that burns but doesn't consume, an undying worm that eats away at the damned, and a lonely, foreboding darkness.

Apologize for this teaching? We should not apologize for Jesus's teaching on eternal punishment. Jesus's first mention of it would appear to be in the Sermon on the Mount. Having referred to the "fire of hell" [Greek: *gehenna*], He goes on to say:

> Everyone who looks at a woman with lustful
> intent has already committed adultery with her in
> his heart. If your right eye causes you to sin, tear
> it out and throw it away. For it is better that you
> lose one of your members than that your whole
> body be thrown into hell. And if your right hand
> causes you to sin, cut it off and throw it away. For
> it is better that you lose one of your members
> than that your whole body go into hell [Greek:
> gehenna].
>
> —MATTHEW 5:28–30

Jesus was using a figure of speech called *hyperbole*; He
was not challenging men literally to pluck their eyes out—
or hundreds would have done that when He finished His
sermon. But He shows His belief in Hell; He means that
it is better to give up things that are precious to you—
painful though this may be—than for your whole being to
be spent in Hell forever.

There are three Greek words that have been translated
Hell at one time or another in various versions of the Bible.
Gehenna, which is connected to fire, is used twelve times
in the New Testament. *Hades*, which means "the grave,"
is also used twelve times in the New Testament, yet when
Jesus referred to *hades* in Luke 16:23–24, it was a place of
fire and torment. A third word, *tartarus*—used only in
2 Peter 2:4—is translated "Hell": "For if God did not spare
angels when they sinned, but cast them into hell and committed them to chains of gloomy darkness to be kept until
the judgment." There are times when Jesus does not use
the word Hell but rather a place of "outer darkness. In that
place there will be weeping and gnashing of teeth" (Matt.

8:12). At the end of the age "angels will come out and separate the evil from the righteous and throw them into
the fiery furnace. In that place there will be weeping and
gnashing of teeth" (Matt. 13:49–50).

A PLACE

Hell is a place as Heaven is a place. Some people would
say that Hell is a state of mind. They speak of "hell on
earth." General Dwight Eisenhower used to say that "war
is hell." Some people would say that "life is hell." It has
become a swear word in the world but seldom used in the
pulpit as it is meant in the Bible. Likewise some would
talk about "heaven on earth." The Puritan Thomas Brooks
(1608—1680) wrote a book he called *Heaven on Earth*.[4] So
yes, either Heaven or Hell may be described as a state of
mind or even as a happy exclamation: "Good heavens!" or
"Heavens to Betsy."

Make no mistake, Heaven is a place. Hell is a place.
Jesus said that a place of "eternal fire" was prepared "for
the devil and his angels." However, it will be a place *not
only* for the devil and his angels. "Then he will say to
those on his left, 'Depart from me, you cursed, into the
eternal fire prepared for the devil and his angels'" (Matt.
25:41). Jesus refers to opposite places of everlasting existence: "And these will go away into eternal punishment,
but the righteous into eternal life" (Matt. 25:46).

These descriptions of Jesus cohere with what Paul
called the revelation of the "wrath of God" (Rom. 1:18).
Being justified by Jesus's blood, "much more shall we be
saved by him from the wrath of God" (Rom. 5:9). Paul

wanted to show the Roman Christians what he believed before he arrived there. He shows what he taught when he was in Thessalonica: we wait the return of God's Son from Heaven, "whom he raised from the dead, Jesus who delivers us from the wrath to come" (1 Thess. 1:10).

If you ask me, Do I like this teaching? No. I wish it weren't true. If God were to leave things to me, I would let everybody out of Hell, save everybody, and do away with eternal punishment altogether. You may recall that in Martin Luther's Ninety-Five Theses he reasoned that if the pope has power over purgatory, why ever doesn't he let everybody out?

In *The Problem of Pain*, C. S. Lewis spoke to those who argue against the doctrine of hell:

> In the long run the answer to all those who object to the doctrine of hell is itself a question: "What are you asking God to do?" To wipe out their past sins and, at all costs, to give them a fresh start, smoothing every difficulty and offering every miraculous help? But he has done so, on Calvary. To forgive them? They will not be forgiven. To leave them alone? Alas, I am afraid that is what he does.[5]

Here is why I teach as I do in this chapter. I am God's ambassador (2 Cor. 5:20). An ambassador faithfully represents and defends the position of his nation's government. He may not personally understand it. He may not always be happy with it. But he defends it. That's me.

ANNIHILATION

Some respected theologians and preachers—and good friends of mine—have opted for the teaching of annihilation. This means that body and soul are annihilated—extinguished, destroyed, or made to disappear—as if they were never created in the first place. Annihilation means that the person ceases to exist. There is an ever-increasing number of respected theologians today who hold this position, far more than there were a generation ago. The number is growing daily.

I recall having lunch with J. I. Packer, probably the most esteemed theologian in the world today, and saying to him, "Guess who now believes in annihilation?"

He replied with dismay, "Who doesn't believe in it these days?" I was glad to learn that he certainly did not believe it, but those who do believe in annihilation are going to be in the majority (I fear) in a short period of time, if not already. Many pastors run fast to this perspective once they learn that highly revered theologians now support it. Esteemed Bible teachers have given the teaching of annihilation a bit of respectability. But thankfully there those who don't believe in it, such as Wayne Grudem. See his *Systematic Theology*.[6] There are men like John Piper and D. A. Carson who do not believe in annihilation but conscious eternal punishment. Thankfully there are many others who have not switched their views from conscious eternal punishment to annihilation. I say this not because I am happy about the teaching of eternal Hell. My utter and sole concern is to be an honest Bible teacher. I don't like being out there by myself! I thank God for those pastors and teachers who are not ashamed to uphold what is without doubt one of the most offensive things to be found in the teachings of Jesus. As for those not wanting to believe in everlasting Hell (who can blame them?), there are two options that I know of:

1. To uphold universalism (that all people will be saved in the end).

2. The theory of annihilation—which mainly the cults such as Jehovah's Witnesses once upheld.

As for the possibility of universalism being true, my chapter on the faith of Christ should be sufficient to deal with this.

SOME IMPLICATIONS FROM BELIEF IN ANNIHILATION

Here's the practical problem with annihilation—apart from it being unbiblical. First, it won't "preach." Those who believe in annihilation (as far as I am able to tell) do not often preach it. (That said, I have to admit sadly that those who do believe in conscious eternal punishment rarely preach it.) It is what they passively hold to—if asked. But the theory of annihilation is not something one often preaches evangelistically as a warning from the wrath to come. It is surely hard to preach annihilation with passion when it is obvious that people's worst fears—eternal punishment—are no longer what they need worry about.

Second, the view of annihilation is giving the person

who rejects the Gospel a theological rationale of what he hoped might be true all along—that there is no Hell to fear. This is what I said to a highly respected friend (now in Heaven) when he shared with me in our home that he had come out publicly for the teaching of annihilation. My reply: "I hope you are right. But I don't think you are. You are handing the unbeliever a theological rationale on a silver platter, what he already is counting on being true." The atheist of course would never believe in Hell, yet to give to him or her the view of annihilation would not stir them in the slightest. It is not going to make them want to believe in God because you are making the God of the Bible seem less "horrible."

Third, it will not restore the fear of God to the church. I happen to believe that there is a correlation between the absence of the fear of God in the church and the absence of belief in eternal punishment. To replace eternal punishment in Hell with annihilation will hardly instill a sense of fear and awe in the hearts of people. The belief in annihilation at best gives a sense of relief—or, sometimes, a measure of respectability—since the traditional teaching on Hell is seen as old-fashioned, dated, ridiculous, and quite out of the question to man "come of age."

One does not come up with the theory of annihilation by a casual, natural reading of the New Testament. For some two thousand years the church generally has taken for granted that Hell is a never-ending punishment. Even the greatest hymn writers have assumed this. For example:

> Where shall my wondering soul begin?
> How shall I all to heaven aspire?

A slave redeemed from death and sin,
A brand plucked from eternal fire,
How shall I equal triumphs raise,
Or sing my great Deliverer's praise?
—CHARLES WESLEY (1707–1788)
"WHERE SHALL MY WONDERING SOUL BEGIN"[7]

The teaching of annihilation is a valiant attempt, consciously or unconsciously, to destigmatize God. I can appreciate those who want to make God "look good." But God does not need a public relations person. Our job is not to make Him look good to the world. We must proclaim Him as He is. This is why Jesus said that the world cannot accept the Holy Spirit (John 14:17). This is the reason that the first work of the Holy Spirit is to convince the world of sin (John 16:7).

One *chooses* to believe in the teaching of annihilation vis-à-vis conscious eternal punishing of the lost. When I say "chooses," it is not because the Scriptures shout "annihilation" to you; quite the opposite. A verse that refers to Hell as "the unquenchable fire" (Mark 9:43) is too plain and too simple to miss. So when Jesus talks about the whole person being thrown into hell, where "their worm does not die and the fire is not quenched" (Mark 9:48), it speaks of never-ending punishment. Why would the fire never go out if those who were there were annihilated? Why the need for eternal fire if there is no one in Hell? Why mention that "utter darkness has been reserved *forever*" (Jude 13, emphasis added)? Or "the smoke of their torment goes up *forever and ever*" (Rev. 14:11, emphasis added)? Or that the devil would be "thrown into the lake of fire" to be "tormented day and night *forever and ever*" (Rev. 20:10, emphasis added)? These verses do not suggest annihilation. The annihilationists seem to be divided on whether Satan will be annihilated. According to Jesus, as I stated, Hell was created for the devil and his angels (Matt. 25:41).

To put it another way: if Jesus and the writers of the New Testament intended to convey the teaching of eternal, conscious punishment, how else could this be *worded* in order for the unbiased reader to believe this is what is being taught?

If one chooses to believe in annihilation, he or she will find "proof" of it in the Bible. We all manage to find verses to support what we want to be true.

One therefore must make a conscious and deliberate choice to believe in annihilation. I do understand this. Those I know who support the teaching of annihilation are good, loving, and conscientious men and women of God. Some are very learned. After all, the historic teaching of Hell is so offensive and annihilation is inoffensive. Once you choose to believe it—knowing that some good and respectable scholars have made this choice first—you will likely be able to prove to yourself that it is actually what the Bible teaches. And it is rather easy to prove—believe it or not!

Two Arguments for the Teaching of Annihilation

I will share two main arguments to support annihilation. The first is to say that the notion of "immortality of the soul" is a Greek idea that has been brought into the Christian faith. The historic Christian view has always been that we are made in the image of God (Gen. 1:27). He is immortal, hence our belief in the immortality of the soul; it is part of being made in the image of God. This means that immortality is a creation gift; it comes with being born. The premise of those who believe in annihilation, however, is this: we are given immortality not by creation but only by regeneration (being born again). In other words, immortality and eternal life are basically identical; we only get such by faith in Jesus Christ. Therefore the person not receiving immortality by faith would not have conscious existence beyond the grave. The problem is that Jesus taught that "all" who are in their graves will be resurrected, some to live and some to "the resurrection of judgment" (John 5:28–29).

There are at least two categories of how a person is annihilated. Some annihilationists believe that the unconverted person ceases to exist when he or she dies— knowing no conscious punishment. They would say that to be annihilated *is* the punishment itself. This means that the impenitent is punished by being deprived of immortality. They would call it eternal punishment because the punishment—annihilation—is permanent. However, most evangelical theologians who are annihilationists believe that the unsaved will have a resurrection in order to face the final judgment. This would mean they are given consciousness to face God but would then would be annihilated.

The second argument I will share in behalf of those who believe in annihilation is the meaning of the Greek word *apolummi*. It is translated "perish" in John 3:16: those who believe in God's one and only Son will "not perish but have eternal life." They take "perish" to mean annihilation. But it is wrong to say that this is what *apolummi* must mean. It can mean "waste." Proof of this: *apolummi* is the word used regarding Jesus's being anointed with a rich perfume. Some objected to using an expensive perfume and asked: "Why this *waste*?" (Matt. 26:8, emphasis added). The perfume was seen as being wasted—but there is no hint of the perfume ceasing to exist. The perfume itself did not disappear. It is like when an insurance company regards a wrecked vehicle as being "totaled"—it is worthless, but all the parts of the automobile are present.

You could waste your life. You can lose your soul. In such a case you certainly would hope that annihilation is true. But it is not true.

Some argue that the apostolic fathers did not teach eternal Hell. But we also have seen that these men sadly had little to say about the doctrines of grace as well! That said, Tertullian (*fl.* AD 200) believed in eternal punishment, and so did St. Augustine.

I learned to debate when I was in high school in 1953. I was on the debate team in my school. To be a good debater, you need to be able to defend both sides. I could— if asked—intellectually defend annihilation. The problem is I don't believe it.

AN UNEXPECTED INSIGHT WHEN
CONDUCTING THE LORD'S SUPPER

Many years ago when conducting the Lord's Supper at Westminster Chapel, I happened to read the scripture that referred to Judas Iscariot—being one of the Twelve and the only disciple who betrayed our Lord. Jesus said of him, "It would be better for that man if he had not been born" (Matt. 26:24). I was not expecting to see what I suddenly saw; I was quickened and gripped. I truly believe it was the Holy Spirit who made me see in that moment what I had never noticed before. In a word, Judas, though he would be eternally lost, would *not* be annihilated. After all, annihilation renders a person nonexistent—as if he had never been born. But Judas was born. It would be better had he not been born, said Jesus. This meant he would not be annihilated. I never looked back after that moment.

I have discussed the subject of eternal punishment with David Gooding of Queen's University Belfast. He is regarded as one of the top Greek scholars in the entire world and a specialist on the *Septuagint*—the Greek translation of the Hebrew Old Testament. He vehemently upholds eternal punishment—if only on the basis of the Greek language. Whereas the annihilationists would claim they do believe in eternal punishment—because annihilation makes the punishment final and permanent— Professor Gooding said to me that technically the Greek used in Matthew 25:46, "these will go away into eternal punishment," could be rightly translated eternal *punishing*—which suggests an ongoing punishment.

THE RICH MAN AND LAZARUS

The scripture I used at the beginning of this chapter is taken from the account of the rich man and Lazarus—one went to Heaven; the other went to Hell. Some say the account is a historical fact; others say it is a parable. It does not matter, although one must not make parables stand evenly on all four legs. (Please see my book *The Parables of Jesus.*[8]) For one thing, the account of the rich man and Lazarus may well refer to the intermediate state (where dead people are between death and the final judgment). If so, it certainly shows that those who die are acutely conscious when they pass on. But that Luke 16:19–31 may refer to the intermediate state would not necessarily change the things we learn about conscious punishment beyond the grave. That said, here are some observations I would make:

1. Jesus did not invent the teaching of Hell; it was an assumption, that is, taken for granted to be true. He did not relate this parable or story to introduce the doctrine of Hell. Therefore when He referred to the rich man being in Hell, although the Greek word is *hades*—the grave—He was saying what the Old Testament taught and what was generally assumed to be true at the time.

2. The rich man was conscious in Hell. There is no hint of annihilation at all.

3. He was in pain—"in torment...I am in anguish in this flame" (Luke 16:23–24).

4. He prayed. "Father Abraham, have mercy on me." This suggests that people will pray in Hell. They will pray essentially the same kind of prayer one prays to become a Christian: "God, be merciful to me, a sinner" (Luke 18:13). But it will be too late to pray in Hell and get your prayer answered.

5. He had his memory. I suspect that one of the things that will make Hell *Hell* is that you will have your memory in Hell. The reply to the rich man was: "Child, remember that you in your lifetime received your good things, and Lazarus in like manner bad things; but now he is comforted here, and you are in anguish" (Luke 16:25). There were other things that could have been said to the rich man. What also will make Hell *Hell*, then, is to be reminded of that which put him or her there. God only punishes when He has reason to do so. The judgment will reveal why one is being consigned to Hell. For example, the Holy Spirit stepped in and judged Ananias and Sapphira for lying to the Holy Spirit. But before they were struck dead, Peter reminded them that they were not required to sell their property—it was theirs; and when they sold the property the money was their own. But because they wanted to be "very in" with those who were selling their property and giving it all to

the apostles, they pretended to do the same thing—but got found out. When Peter then told them they had not lied to men but to God, they were struck dead (Acts 5:1–10).

6. The rich man was apparently alone. People sometimes glibly say, "If I go to Hell, I will have a lot of company." Chances are, you would not be aware of such company. Besides, they could not give you the slightest comfort.

7. It is permanent. "And beside all this, between us and you a great chasm has been fixed, in order that those who would pass from here to you may not be able, and none may cross from there to us" (Luke 16:26).

8. The only proof that you are going to get that Hell actually exists is what the Bible teaches about it. The rich man pleaded that Lazarus be sent to convince his five brothers that Hell is real. If Lazarus were to be raised from the dead, presumably his five brothers would be convinced. The reply: "They have Moses and the Prophets; let them hear them" (v. 29), and then came these solemn words: "If they [the five brothers] do not hear Moses and the Prophets, neither will they be convinced if someone should rise from the dead" (v. 31).

IS THE FIRE LITERAL OR FIGURATIVE LANGUAGE?

If you ask, "Is the fire in Hell literal, physical, or is it beyond anything we can imagine?" I don't know. Perhaps it is the same fire that Moses saw when the burning bush was not consumed (Exod. 3:2–3). That was a supernatural fire. Whatever it is—literal, physical, spiritual, allegorical, figurative, or hyperbole—I stand with Abraham: "Shall not the Judge of all the earth do what is just?" (Gen. 18:25). That question settles it for me because the answer is *yes*—God is just, fair, righteous, and infinitely wise. Whatever God Almighty decides will be right and *seen as right*.

One further observation: We have no idea who the rich man was; we don't even know his name. But we know the name of the man who went to Heaven—Lazarus. God said to Israel, "Fear not, for I have redeemed you; I have called you by *name*, you are mine" (Isa. 43:1, emphasis added). Jesus said to the seventy-two whom He sent two by two to every town and place where He was about to go, "Rejoice that your *names* are written in heaven" (Luke 10:20, emphasis added).

When I was a boy we used to sing this hymn:

> Is my name written there,
> On the page white and fair?
> In the book of Thy kingdom,
> Is my name written there?
> —MARY A. KIDDER (1820–1905)
> "IS MY NAME WRITTEN THERE?"[9]

A Wonderful Assurance

All day long on that memorable day in my own life—October 31, 1955—I rejoiced with unspeakable relief that I knew I was eternally saved. I cannot come close to describing the relief I felt all day long: I will not be going to Hell. When hundreds fell to the ground under the power of the Holy Spirit at the Cane Ridge Revival in 1802, when the preacher spoke from 2 Corinthians 5:10: "For we must all appear before the judgment seat of Christ, so that each one may receive what is due for what he has done in the body, whether good or evil," the same people hours later came out of it shouting. The fear of the Lord had fallen on the people. But when they came up with assurance, their voices were raised to a high level. It was reported to be like "the sound of Niagara"—hundreds and hundreds of people shouting could be heard a mile away. It was the relief that came that one is saved and not lost. The assumption of Hell pervaded the preaching and the perception of the people. Their relief that they would not be eternally lost in Hell was incalculable.

For some the reaction may be, "I never worried about going to Hell in the first place." I understand that. But you should worry. What I have written in this book is true. Hell is real. Heaven is real. The devil does not want you to believe this. In the same way that Satan tries to distort and pervert the Gospel, so also will he divert people from thinking about Hell.

I will say again that it is my opinion that the absence of the fear of God in the church generally is partly traceable to the lack of preaching and belief in Hell. There is a strong correlation between the lack of the fear of God in the land and the absence of belief in Hell in the church.

The good news is Hell is a place where no one need go. *You don't need to go there.* Nothing can be more thrilling than this—that we know our "names" are written in Heaven. That means we are not going to Hell.

WHY DIDN'T THE GOSPEL WRITERS EXPLAIN HELL?

Have you ever thought of the times Jesus willingly allowed Himself to be misunderstood—and never bothered to explain himself? He said things that were quite ridiculous on the surface and made no effort to say, "Sorry, I didn't mean to say that." Or, "Let me rephrase what I said." Or, "What I really meant was..." In other words, there were occasions when the people thought one thing, but Jesus meant another, and He did not bother to explain what He actually meant. For example, when Jesus said to His critics, "Destroy this temple, and in three days I will raise it up" (John 2:19), He knew exactly how this was perceived, that He surely referred to the temple in Jerusalem. He let Himself be misunderstood. "It has taken forty-six years to build this temple," they replied, "and you will raise it up in three days?" (v. 20). Indeed, this statement was used against Him when the Jews were looking for ammunition to warrant His crucifixion. "'This man said, "I am able to destroy the temple of God, and to rebuild it in three days."' And the high priest stood up and said, 'Have you no answer to make? What is it that these men testify against you?' *But Jesus remained silent*" (Matt. 26:61–63, emphasis added).

It was not until John wrote the Fourth Gospel many years later that Jesus's real meaning was explained: "But he was speaking about the temple of his body" (John 2:21). After He "was raised from the dead, his disciples remembered that he had said this" (v. 22). Years later John chose to explain what Jesus actually meant. Jesus did not explain Himself; John did.

However, on other occasions the writers of the gospels do not "put the record straight" or say, "Here is what Jesus really meant," when Jesus said things that were very offensive. For example, in John chapter 6—which contains some of the "hard sayings" of the Gospel—Jesus called Himself "the bread that came down from heaven" (v. 41). He made no attempt to explain what He meant. He allowed His enemies to verbalize what had been rumored for years— that Jesus was the illegitimate son of Joseph and Mary. "Is not this Jesus, the son of Joseph, whose father and mother we know? How does he now say, 'I have come down from heaven'?" (v. 42). The proof that they were referring to Jesus's alleged birth out of wedlock came when they said, "We be not born of fornication" (John 8:41, KJV). It was as though they were saying, "Unlike you, Jesus, we are not illegitimate children." No one cared about these rumors as long as Jesus was feeding thousands from the loaves and fish. But once He said things that were way out of their comfort zone, they began to show their hatred of Jesus. Neither did John later inject a word, "Oh, by the way, Jesus was actually born of the Virgin Mary." The account of the virgin birth is not even found in John.

You can be sure that if the Jews generally were aware of these ugly rumors, so too were the twelve disciples. But they were loyal nonetheless and did not question Jesus. There is no indication that the twelve knew about the Virgin Mary giving birth to Jesus. The disclosure of how the Son of God was born emerged years later when Mary gave Luke the details, and Matthew too was given this information. As I said, no one cared about these rumors as long as Jesus was feeding thousands from the loaves and fish.

The question is, Do we have a right to pick and choose which statements of Jesus we want to believe?

And yet there is more. Jesus said, "Whoever feeds on my flesh and drinks my blood has eternal life, and I will raise him up on the last day. For my flesh is true food, and my blood is true drink" (John 6:54–55). That did it. On hearing this, even many of His followers said, "This is a hard saying. Who can listen to it?" (v. 60) and "no longer walked with him" (v. 66). That was possibly the most obnoxious thing of all to His hearers. John might have, but did not bother to explain that this was a reference to the Lord's Supper.

In other words, sometimes John explained some things Jesus said but left other of His statements alone.

Yet surely one of the most offensive and difficult teachings of Jesus is that of conscious eternal punishment. It would have been nice for all of us had John helped us to grasp this teaching by some comment so that we might not be perplexed by it. But no. There was no apology from any of the gospel writers about Jesus's teaching of eternal punishment.

When Jesus finished the hard sayings in John 6, noting that thousands stopped following Him, He said to the twelve: "'Do you not want to go away as well?' Simon Peter answered him, 'Lord, to whom shall we go? You have the words of eternal life, and we have believed and have come to know, that you are the Holy One of God'" (vv. 67–68).

I ask you, the reader: When you hear of offensive teaching—especially that regarding eternal punishment, are you going to back off from following Jesus? Or will you say, "To whom shall we go? Jesus is the one and only Son of God"?

Hell is God's idea. Not mine. His ways are higher than our ways; His thoughts, higher than our thoughts. Indeed, "As the heavens are higher than the earth, so are my ways higher than your ways and my thoughts than your thoughts," says the Lord (Isa. 55:9). However wrong, ridiculous, and unfair this teaching may seem to you and me, we should lower our voices and side, as I said before, with Abraham. He too could not understand why God would destroy Sodom and Gomorrah without giving them a minute's warning but resigned himself with this question: "Shall not the Judge of all the earth do what is just?" (Gen. 18:25). That's where I am when I cannot take this teaching in.

A friend of mine who had opted for the teaching of annihilation gave me a loving slap on the wrist and asked me, "Why, RT, make such an issue over something peripheral?"

I replied, "But what if it's true? What if there really is a Hell? What if there really is a Hell, as I have taught? In that case it is certainly *not* peripheral." He nodded agreement.

You will recall the story of Charlie Stride toward the beginning of this book. He was a taxi driver with no church background whatever. When he read my tract

"What Is Christianity?" he was shaken from head to toe. Why? It was because the Holy Spirit, who wrote the Bible, came alongside Charlie and gave him a glimpse of eternity. That is what happened on July 8, 1741, when people held on to church pews and tree trunks to keep from sliding into Hell. For reasons I do not understand, the Holy Spirit does not seem to intervene like this every day. But when He does, it is because a sovereign, just, and merciful God has chosen to step in and convict a person of judgment to come. My only hope of reaching you in this book is that the same Holy Spirit will apply these words to you.

If we don't meet here below, I pray that I will see you in Heaven.

CHAPTER TWELVE

HEAVEN

In my Father's house are many rooms. If it were not so, would I have told you that I go to prepare a place for you? And if I go and prepare a place for you, I will come again and will take you to myself, that where I am you may be also.
—JOHN 14:2–3

ONE OF THE most amazing facts of American history is that many black slaves in the Deep South became Christians. When you consider the cruelty, the injustices, and the pain of these men and women, brought on by their white owners, it is extraordinary that any of these slaves would become Christians. Yet many did.

Why? It was mainly the idea of Heaven that appealed to them. That got their attention. When the preachers mentioned the hope of Heaven in the next life, their ears perked up. The thought that there would be an end of pain, grief, injustice, and unfairness sat well with these mistreated people. If there is a place called Heaven, they were interested. Sitting in the segregated balconies of churches in Georgia, Alabama, and Mississippi and listening to preaching, these slaves were given something to live for. Out of the Deep South came some of our most precious hymns, spirituals, and choruses:

- "Swing Low, Sweet Chariot"
- "Deep River"
- "Nobody Knows the Troubles I've Seen"
- "I'll Fly Away, Oh Glory"
- "I Got Shoes, You Got Shoes"
- "Roll, Jordan, Roll"
- "There Must Be a Heaven Somewhere"

When Jesus refers to His Father's "house" in John 14:2, it is a euphemism referring to Heaven. The King James Version states, "In my Father's house are many mansions." That translation gave rise to the widespread feeling that we will live in a mansion when we get to Heaven. I grew up hearing this song, which was later made popular by Elvis Presley (1935–1977):

> I've got a mansion just over the hilltop,
> In that bright land where we'll never grow old;
> And some day yonder we will never more wander,
> But walk on streets that are purest gold.
> —IRA STANPHILL (1914–1993)
> "MANSION OVER THE HILLTOP"[1]

Most versions of John 14:2 translate the Greek *monai* as rooms or dwellings: "In my Father's house are many rooms." Whatever the exact meaning, it shows that the Lord is preparing a *place* with many dwellings for us to live in. As I said earlier, Heaven is a place. It is not a state of mind but a place.

Paul used a euphemism for Heaven too, although he was referring to the intermediate state: "For we know that if the tent that is our earthly home is destroyed, we have a building from God, a house not made with hands, eternal in the heavens" (2 Cor. 5:1). He is referring to a temporary spiritual body one gets when he or she dies. However, we will be given glorified bodies at the second coming of Jesus.

When I speak of Heaven in this chapter, I am going to pass over certain eschatological details as to the order of events pertaining to the time and manner of Jesus's second coming. (I touched on this briefly in *Prepare Your Heart for the Midnight Cry.*[2]) I only want to speak of Heaven, as we will inherit it down the road—what Jesus promised to prepare for us.

These things said, we will all learn a lot more about Heaven five minutes after we are there than all the preaching, guessing, imagining, writing, and fantasizing might suggest this side of Heaven. I write this final but important chapter based upon what limited knowledge I have—derived from Holy Scripture, but combined with a bit of benign sanctified speculation. Forty years ago I was asked by a publisher to write a book on Heaven. I welcomed the invitation. But I never finished the manuscript. I soon realized I do not know enough to write a book on Heaven. The nearest I have come is this very chapter.

What follows is but a drop in the bucket compared with what needs to be written.

HEAVEN IS A PLACE

In John 14:2 Jesus said He was going to His Father's house to prepare a *place* for His followers. I have emphasized that Hell is a place, not a state of mind. So too Heaven is a place, which Jesus promised to prepare. He has had plenty of time preparing this place! He could have done it perfectly in a split second, but after two thousand years—oh dear!

The writer of Hebrews called it the "world to come" (Heb. 2:5). It is also called a "city." Abraham was looking forward to "the *city* that has foundations, whose designer and builder is God" (Heb. 11:10, emphasis added). God so affirmed those men and women who lived by faith that He "is not ashamed to be called their God, for he has prepared for them a *city*" (v. 16). "For here we have no lasting city, but we seek the *city* that is to come" (Heb. 13:14).

I take that city to be the New Jerusalem as described by John:

> And I saw the holy city, new Jerusalem, coming down out of heaven from God, prepared as a bride adorned for her husband. And I heard a loud voice from the throne saying, "Behold, the dwelling place of God is with man. He will dwell with them, and they will be his people, and God himself will be with them as their God."
>
> —REVELATION 21:2–3

Whatever will Heaven be like? I have to say that we are told more about what will *not* be in Heaven than what is in Heaven. (But what is not there makes it awfully good!) We are told more about what we will *not* be doing in Heaven than what we will be doing in Heaven. You must remember that Heaven is a God-centered place, one in which the Lamb of God is the absolute focus. Questions such as "Will God give me a horse in Heaven?" "Will I get to go fishing in Heaven?" "Will there be a golf course in Heaven?" "Will we visit the planets in Heaven?" or "Will I go shopping in Heaven?" hardly come into the Book of Revelation!

Someone asked the quaint and eccentric Uncle Buddy Robinson (1860–1942), "Can a feller go to Heaven who chews tobacco?"

Uncle Buddy replied, "He'd have to go to Hell to spit!"

I have had not a few people suggest to me that Heaven sounds boring if all we will do is worship. To be fair, I can see what people mean by that. But I can assure you, that won't be a problem. First, we will have glorified bodies. None of us knows what that will be like. Second, we will have vastly different perspectives when we get there. We will be God-centered in our thoughts, words, and deeds. Third, to be able to worship the Lord Jesus Christ with our very eyes will be so thrilling and glorious that it will not come into one's mind to do anything else. God Himself will certainly decide what else we might do throughout the countless years of eternity.

There are some things we can be fairly sure of however.

1. Heaven is a place of restoration of what was lost in the Fall and in the Garden of Eden.

Peter said that Jesus will remain at the right hand of the Father "until the time for restoring all the things about which God spoke by the mouth of his holy prophets long ago" (Acts 3:21). He who was seated on the throne said, "I am making all things new!" (Rev. 21:5).

In the middle of the Garden of Eden there was the tree of life and the tree of the knowledge of good and evil (Gen. 2:9). But John makes no mention of the tree of the knowledge of good and evil in Heaven. He said:

> Then the angel showed me the river of the water of life, bright as crystal, flowing from the throne of God and of the Lamb through the middle of the street of the city; also, on either side of the river, the tree of life with its twelve kinds of fruit, yielding its fruit each month. The leaves of the tree were for the healing of the nations.
> —REVELATION 22:1–2

We all are curious to know more about what will be in Heaven and what we will see in Heaven. We would all like to know more regarding what we will be *doing* in Heaven. Yet enough is indicated to demonstrate that the Garden of Eden will be restored. And the reference to the "healing of the nations" is fascinating. Who knows what all that means. But it is an indication that Heaven will be a place of peace. There will be no more wars.

The reference to fruit does suggest that we will be eating in Heaven. But fruit is all that is mentioned. This may come as a disappointment to those of us who can only envision eating a steak or smoked salmon as something really exciting—or chicken tikka masala! But I can guarantee this: you will be more than satisfied.

In Heaven we will worship as Adam did before the Fall—but with this glorious exception: we will have something to be thankful for that Adam would know nothing about. There was no sin in Adam before the Fall, so he worshipped without the weight and heaviness of sin. But in Heaven we will worship not only without sin but also with overflowing gratitude:

> And they sang a new song, saying, "Worthy are you to take the scroll and open its seals, for you were slain, and by your blood you ransomed people for God from every tribe and language and people and nation."
>
> —REVELATION 5:9

2. It is a place where all the people of God who ever lived will dwell.

There will be no child of God absent in Heaven. Every child of God who ever lived will be present. The gates of Heaven will not be closed until every person who has been born again is welcomed in. Every person who has been justified by faith will be there. Every person who has been adopted into the family of God will be there. In other words, all of God's chosen people will be there—those whose sins have been washed by the blood of the Lamb.

The number of people that will be in Heaven will be so great that "no one can count" the number. That's a lot of people! Every person in the history of humankind who was redeemed by the blood of Jesus Christ will be present.

They will come from every century, every generation, every year in the history of the human race. They will come from every tribe, language, people, and nation (Rev. 5:9). They will come from every state of every country. Although we will all speak the same language, every language that was on the earth will be represented. Every accent of every language will be represented. Those people from Kentucky, Holland, or Wales who thought their tongue was the "language of Heaven" will learn to speak the same new language of this countless multitude!

3. It will be a holy place.

"Nothing unclean will ever enter it, nor anyone who does what is detestable or false, but only those who are written in the Lamb's book of life" (Rev. 21:27). The most holy God, who is "of purer eyes than to see evil and cannot look at wrong" (Hab. 1:13), will guarantee that Heaven is devoid of the slightest taint or hint of sin. The God of the Bible had commanded ancient Israel, "Be holy, for I am holy" (Lev. 11:44). Likewise He commanded His redeemed people to be holy (1 Pet. 1:16).

Therefore Heaven will be a holy place. There will be no one selling drugs, no one indulging in prostitution or pornography. There will be no wicked music that is inspired by Satan and the demonic world. There will be no lying, cheating, betraying, infidelity, or dishonesty. There will be no miscarriages of justice, no bribery, no evil judges, and no crooked politicians. There will be no idolatry, witchcraft, astrology charts, or fortunetellers. No unfaithfulness in marriage. No marriage separations. No divorces.

No adultery. No fornication. No sexual perversion. No raping. No kidnapping. No abuse. No mistreatment.

There will be no policemen in Heaven. No sheriffs. No corrupt judges. There will be no lawlessness in Heaven. No crooked lawyers who get rich people off the hook but show contempt for the poor person. There will be no injustices in Heaven when the well-connected are protected but the person with no money or connections goes to prison. There will be no jails in Heaven. No prisons in Heaven.

4. It will be a place where all the residents have been glorified.

Glorification is described by the apostle Paul as the fourth and final stage in the golden chain of redemption: predestination, calling, justification, and glorification. "Those whom he predestined he also called, and those he called he also justified, and those whom he justified he also glorified" (Rom. 8:30).

Every person in Heaven will be like Jesus. That does not mean we will look exactly like Him. Or that we will be aged thirty-three. Or that we will have His color of eyes. Or have His brain. Or His IQ. It means we will be without sin and will have bodies without any defect. Each person will have his or her same identity in Heaven as he or she had on earth. We shall know as we are known (1 Cor. 13:12). The disciples recognized Moses and Elijah on the Mount of Transfiguration (Matt. 17:2). So too will Jesus look the same as He did in His days on earth. He will have the same Middle Eastern complexion, same color of hair, same color of eyes, same eyebrows, same nose size, and same height that He had when He died on the cross at the age of thirty-three. His resurrection from the dead did not change His looks. He was the same Jesus whom His followers had seen and known but with scars on His body and in His hands (John 20:25–27). He is the only person in Heaven who will have any scars or blemishes on His body. Throughout eternity Jesus will have those scars. They will remind us forever and ever how it was we got to Heaven in the first place—by His horrible death on the cross.

So when I say that everybody will be like Jesus, I refer therefore not to outward appearance but to the matter of sinlessness. Whom God foreknew He predestined "to be conformed to the image of his Son, in order that he might be the firstborn among many brothers" (Rom. 8:29). "We shall be like him, because we shall see him as he is" (1 John 3:2). We will have been "changed" from mortality to immortality, from corruption to incorruption (1 Cor. 15:52–53). We will be made like Christ's "glorious body" (Phil. 3:21).

Frances Jane van Alstyne, better known as Fanny Crosby (1820–1915), is one of the greatest hymn writers of all time. She wrote possibly eight thousand hymns and gospel songs. She developed an eye infection at the age of six weeks. The treatment that was used damaged her optic nerve, and she became blind from that time. Someone who tried to sympathize said to her, "I feel so sorry that you have never seen the light of day or any person around you." Her reply: "Don't you realize that the first sight I ever see will be the face of Jesus?" She wrote this hymn:

Someday the silver cord will break,
And I no more as now shall sing;

But, oh, the joy when I shall wake
Within the palace of the king!

And I shall see Him face to face,
And tell the story—Saved by grace.

—FANNY CROSBY
"SAVED BY GRACE"[3]

There will be no blindness in Heaven. There will be no disease in Heaven. No illness. No sickness. No one will be in a wheelchair. No one will be walking with canes or on crutches. There will no one limping from muscular dystrophy. Nobody will be weak from multiple sclerosis. There will be no one wearing hearing aids. We will not need glasses. No one will be malnourished; no one will suffer from being overweight. There will be no heart disease, no need for stents or heart bypasses. No one will suffer from breathing difficulties. No one will suffer from memory loss or concentration problems. No allergies. No coughing. No sneezing. There will be no one with digestive problems, no kidney or bladder issues, no sore throats or sinus infections. No cancer. There will be no learning disabilities; no one with backaches; no one with hip, knee, or feet difficulties. There will be no lack of strength from old age, no one who will be bedfast or needing to be fed. There will be no teeth issues, no cavities, no toothaches, no tooth implants.

There will be no need for dentists in Heaven. No need for physicians in Heaven. No surgeons. No medical consultants. No filled waiting rooms for doctors' appointments. No ambulances. There will be no need for health insurance. There will be no psychiatrists, psychologists, or marriage counselors.

To be glorified, then, will mean that we will have perfect bodies. Perfect minds. Perfect eyes. Perfect hearing. Perfect posture. No weakness. No tiredness. No need for sleep!

This means therefore that we will be sinless. That is one of the most important aspects of glorification. There will be no corruption or deceit in us. In this life the heart is deceitful and incurable above all things (Jer. 17:9), but all of the natural depravity inherited from Adam will be totally eradicated—annihilated. The only annihilation I believe in is the nonexistence of sin and temptation! There will be no jealousy or envy. No vanity. No proud looks. No competitiveness. No one-upmanship. No lusting. No coveting. No hate. No anger. No bitterness. No unforgiveness. No grudges. No need for vindication. No need to be noticed. No desire for recognition or getting the credit for a good deed. No desire to get even. No need to clear your name. No dishonesty, untruthfulness, or betrayal. No need to prove yourself.

I cannot imagine remotely what this will be like. I could not possibly know what an existence without inward sin and without the susceptibility to temptation would be like. Jesus was without sin yet was tempted (Heb. 4:15). But in Heaven there will be no sinful nature, neither will there be any temptation. Think on this: we will be inwardly sinless like Jesus and having nothing in Heaven to tempt us! The thought is too mind-boggling to figure out.

5. It will be a place where there are no financial worries.

No one will be in debt. There will be no bill collectors. No last warning notices in the post to pay your bill. There will be no need for savings accounts. There will be no lawyers. No solicitors. No barristers. No judges. No wrong or unjust verdicts. No monthly payments for mortgages. No water bills. No electric bills. No heating bills. No medical bills. No dentist bills. No anxiety over what to wear. No upward mobility issues. No envy over wealth, expensive cars, huge homes, or prestigious locations. No boasting of a great salary. No need to show off your home.

6. There will be no sadness in Heaven.

God "will wipe every tear" from our eyes. There will be no funerals in Heaven. No goodbyes. No sorrow. No pain. "And death shall be no more, neither shall there be mourning, nor crying, nor pain anymore, for the former things have passed away" (Rev. 21:4). No grief over a lost loved one—whether a child, mother, father, brother, sister, close friend. There will be no undertakers, no morticians in Heaven. There will be no need for pastoral care for grieving people over their loss. There will be no weeping for grief, no weeping for pain, no weeping over disappointment, rejection, or loneliness in Heaven. Whereas there can be unspeakable loneliness in a crowd, the countless billions in Heaven will be true friends who will never betray or reject you. For all will be like Jesus—a person whose heart went out to lonely people. The matter of loneliness will come to an end the first second we enter Heaven.

7. It will be a place of continual worship.

We have a glimpse of this in the Book of Revelation. The four living creatures day or night "never cease to say":

> Holy, holy, holy is the Lord God Almighty, who was and is and is to come!
> —REVELATION 4:8

The one difference between Isaiah seeing the glory of God in his day and seeing it once we are in Heaven will be that we will not be convicted of any sin. There will be no sin to be convicted of! No sense of sin will be possible. All depravity and deceitfulness of heart will be forever removed. Seeing Jesus will solve that! We shall be like Him. When Isaiah saw the cherubim and the glory of God, he lamented, "Woe is me! For I am lost" (Isa. 6:5). But not when we get to Heaven. There will be no conviction of sin, therefore, because we will have no sin nature. We cannot even be tempted. We will be utterly unable to sin. St. Augustine posed four stages of all humankind:

1. Man was created *able to sin*.

2. After the Fall man was *unable not to sin*.

3. After regeneration man was *able not to sin*.

4. After glorification man will be *not able to sin*![4]

There will be no temptation to worship a false god. There will be no idols. No Baals. No false religions. No Buddhism. No Islam. No Shintoism. No pictures of saints. No pictures of Jesus. No pictures of angels. No icons. No wandering of the mind when trying to worship. No need to get quiet in order to get into the proper mood to worship. Our glorified bodies and spirits and minds will need no preparation; we will enter into spontaneous praise and worship. We won't be doing it to "bring Heaven down"; we will be *in* Heaven and right in the middle of the highest level of praise that ever was.

In my book *Worshipping God* I suggest that we can learn from the angels on how to worship.[5] They are sinless beings and perhaps have been unparalleled examples of proper worship. They never focus on themselves. They don't want any attention. They are focused on God. That said, we will outdo the angels when we get to Heaven. As one great hymn writer put it:

> Holy, holy is what the angels sing,
> And I expect to help them make the courts of
>   Heaven ring;
> But when I sing redemption's story, they will fold
>   their wings,
> For angels never felt the joys that our salvation
>   brings.
> —JOHN OATMAN JR. (1856–1922)
> "HOLY, HOLY IS WHAT THE ANGELS SING"[6]

There will be no praying in Heaven. There will be no intercession in Heaven. There will be no faith in Heaven. "Faith is the assurance of things hoped for, the conviction of things not seen" (Heb. 11:1). Faith, then, is believing without seeing. But in Heaven you will see! The secular atheist says, "I will believe it when I see it." The problem with that is, if you see it, it is not faith! You will need no faith in Heaven. All will be clear and visible. No need to trust God for this or that. No prayer requests will be shared in Heaven. If you want to pray, do it now. If you want a desire for a closer walk with God, draw nigh to Him now; there will be no need for this in Heaven. If you want time with God alone, do it now. If you want intimacy with the Holy Spirit, start now. Prayer time will be over. No need for quiet time. One of the most moving lines in all hymnody is the final verse of the hymn "Sweet Hour of Prayer":

> Sweet hour of prayer! Sweet hour of prayer!
> May I Thy consolation share,
> Till, from Mount Pisgah's lofty height,
> I view my home and take my flight.
> This robe of flesh I'll drop, and rise
> To seize the everlasting prize,
> And shout, while passing through the air,
> "Farewell, farewell, sweet hour of prayer!"
> —WILLIAM W. WALFORD (1772–1850)
> "SWEET HOUR OF PRAYER"[7]

Charles Wesley longed for "a thousand tongues to sing" God's praise; he longed for a heart to praise his God and for a heart from sin set free. Whatever will it be like when the total population of Heaven becomes one great choir—a multitude that no man can number—with voices singing and making a sound that no human being could now imitate? But who knows what that will be like.

Heaven will be a noisy place. There were "loud voices in heaven," which said:

> The kingdom of the world has become the
> kingdom of our Lord and of his Christ, and he
> shall reign forever and ever.
>
> —REVELATION 11:15

I am sure of this. Worship will be God-centered. It will be solely to exalt Jesus Christ. No human being will want attention. No worship leader will want to draw attention to himself or herself. No composer will have a need to write a better song—whether greater words or original tunes.

I don't know if there will be preaching in Heaven—unless it is to proclaim the glories of the Father, Son, and Holy Spirit. But this much is for sure: there will be no soul-winning in Heaven. Everybody there has been saved. There will be no tithing in Heaven. For some there has been no tithing on earth! There will be no giving to the poor in Heaven. No one will need your money. There could be teaching in Heaven—very possibly. I look forward to learning. But there will be no need for a teacher with a huge ego to say something that has not been said before—no need to be original! Whereas a sign of the last days would be that people will be learning but *never able* to come to the truth (2 Tim. 3:7), I think that in Heaven we will be ever learning but *able* to grasp and rejoice in truth. There will be no difficult verses unexplained, no truth that is too profound, no false theories. There will be no heresies in Heaven.

I admit to a measure of speculation in this chapter. But I reckon that we will not only get our questions answered but see where we got it wrong in our opinions.

As for God clearing His name by answering the question

"Why does He allow suffering and evil?" that will be answered at the judgment seat of Christ. I deal with this in my book *Totally Forgiving God*.[8] Habakkuk's question, Why does God allow evil and suffering? (Hab. 2:13), will be fully and totally answered on the day that every knee shall bow and every tongue confess that Jesus Christ is Lord to the glory of God the Father (Phil. 2:9–11).

I reckon also that God will let us see what went on in the years and centuries prior to our time—up close. Imagine a giant DVD (or something like that) that takes us right back to the sight of:

- Creation
- The Fall
- Abraham attempting to sacrifice Isaac
- The Passover and the Israelites crossing the Red Sea on dry land
- Elijah calling the fire down on Mount Carmel
- The birth of Jesus, the kings and the shepherds
- Jesus preaching the Sermon on the Mount
- The crucifixion of Jesus—and what He went through
- The resurrection of Jesus
- Pentecost and Peter's sermon

- Paul in prison and writing his epistles
- John on the isle of Patmos

We will clearly see events in church history:

- Polycarp dying at the stake
- The formation of the canon of Scripture
- Athanasius standing alone for the deity of Jesus Christ
- Martin Luther nailing his Ninety-Five Theses in Wittenberg
- Nicholas Ridley and Hugh Latimer dying at the stake
- George Whitefield preaching
- John Wesley preaching
- Jonathan Edwards's "Sinners in the Hands of an Angry God"
- The Cane Ridge Revival
- The Azusa Street Revival in Los Angeles
- Any event in history or church history we may want to visit

We will personally meet the great men and women of the Bible—and great people in history—in Heaven. All of them. I want to meet Paul the apostle. I will ask him, "Did I faithfully interpret what you said about the faith of Christ?" I want to ask James, "Did I really get it right on your epistle in James 2:14?" I want to meet Martin Luther—my hero. John Calvin—my favorite theologian. Charles Wesley and John Newton—my favorite hymn writers. Martyn Lloyd-Jones—my chief mentor.

One of the things I expect to be true is the reunion with our loved ones. My mother has been there since 1953, my father since 2002. I have friends I want to see there. All my mentors who have shaped my mind and preaching style.

But first and foremost—words fail me to put this as I would wish...I only know...I WANT TO SEE JESUS! *The wonderful thing is that we will get to see Him before we see anyone else.* I want to worship Him. To thank Him for leaving Heaven, to become nothing, to make Himself of no reputation, to become an embryo in the Virgin Mary's womb. I want to thank Him for fulfilling the Law. For never sinning. For dying on the cross. For saving me. I will thank Him for His infinite patience with me. I am sure I speak for you too! I hope so! It would be unthinkably horrible to miss Heaven. And you do not need to miss it.

Here is the truth: Heaven is real. "Write this down," said the angel to John, "These words are trustworthy and true" (Rev. 21:5). The Bible is the infallible Word of God; it is God's integrity put on the line. His integrity, His Word, His honor, and His glory are at stake.

8. Heaven is a place where there is no darkness but always light.

It is the opposite of what is satanic. Opposite of evil. Jesus said that men loved darkness rather than light because their deeds are evil (John 3:18). But "God is light, and in him is no darkness at all" (1 John 1:5). There is such brilliance of light in Heaven that the sun is not necessary. The apostle Paul reported that when he was struck down on the road to Damascus he saw a light from heaven "brighter than the sun" (Acts 26:13). John saw the glorified Christ on the isle of Patmos and testified that His *face* was "like the sun shining in full strength" (Rev. 1:16). As for Heaven itself, John said it had no need of the moon or sun for light because "the glory of God gives it light, and its lamp is the Lamb" (Rev. 21:23).

9. Heaven is a place that will last forever.

Do you know the feeling of going somewhere on vacation and wishing you could stay on and on and on? Everything is so pleasant, so restful, so beautiful. We used to go to the Florida Keys every summer when I was at Westminster Chapel. I was always so excited to begin bonefishing on Largo Sound in Key Largo. I would think, "Today is the first day..." It was always so good to be at the *beginning* of a vacation. But you knew it would end.

I wonder what it will be like the first day in Heaven! Will we be pinching ourselves every day, trying to take it in that it will last forever? It will surely seem too good to be true. When we've been there ten thousand years, we've no less days to sing God's praise! Try to take that in.

10. Heaven is home.

"Our citizenship is in heaven," said Paul (Phil. 3:20). When you have lived in dozens of places in the world, as Louise and I have in fifty-nine years of marriage, you do not know where to call home! At the time of writing this book, we spend about six months in London and six months in Tennessee. I once asked Jackie Pullinger, "Where is home for you?" She looked at me and pointed upward to the sky. "And I really do mean that," she added. I believe her. I truly do feel the same way.

One cannot go back home here on the earth in any case. Several years ago I took my family to Hilton Avenue in Ashland, Kentucky. The old house did not remotely look the same. The big cherry tree in the front yard was gone. Nothing in the backyard was the same. The front porch of our old house was gone. It was such a disappointment. But we can't go home in any case.

When I was a teenager, I sang in a quartet. We called ourselves "The King David Quartet." One of the songs we sang in those days was this:

> This world is not my home, I'm just a-passing
>   through;
> My treasures are laid up somewhere beyond the
>   blue;
> The angels beckon me from heaven's open door,
> And I can't feel at home in this world anymore.
> —ALBERT EDWARD BRUMLEY (1905–1977)
> "THIS WORLD IS NOT MY HOME"[9]

God doesn't want us to feel at home here below. Have you wondered why you still have trials and tribulations? Financial problems? Health problems? Has it occurred to you that if you got all you wanted here below you would become too enamored with the things of this earth?

God wants you to fix your eyes on that city that Abraham envisaged. He was never allowed to feel at home in this world. Are you having trouble adjusting to this world? Congratulations! God is treating you as He did Abraham. Pretty good company, I would say. As for the first day in Heaven, I think of this line from the hymn "When We All Get to Heaven":

> Just one glimpse of Him in glory
> will the toils of life repay.
> > —ELIZA E. HEWITT (1801–1900)
> > "WHEN WE ALL GET TO HEAVEN"[10]

Or consider these words:

> It will be worth it all when we see Jesus,
> Life's trials will seem so small when we see
> > Christ;
> One glimpse of His dear face all sorrows will
> > erase,
> So bravely run the race till we see Christ.
> > —ESTHER KERR RUSTHOI (1909–1962)
> > "WHEN WE SEE CHRIST"[11]

CONCLUSION

S OMETIME AFTER MARTIN Luther King Jr. was assas-
sinated, when I was pastor of the Lauderdale Manors
Baptist Church in Fort Lauderdale, Florida, I invited
the senior pastor from the Mount Olivet Baptist Church—
a black church nearby—to preach for us. I did this partly
to show solidarity with him and his church at a time when
there was a lot of racial unrest. He brought his choir along.
The singing was magnificent. It was an unforgettable evening. The pastor's sermon was amazing. All were aware
that racial tensions were high. In his sermon the elderly
pastor noted that many preachers had more or less moved
away from preaching the Gospel and were stressing issues
such as social justice. The emphasis was away from the
subject of Heaven and emphasizing life in the here and
now. The traditional Gospel of Christ was on the brink of
disappearing in many places, he said, especially from black
pulpits. The old black pastor began to soar with eloquence
as he began to quote some of the old spirituals to which
I referred at the beginning of the chapter on Heaven in
this book. His sermon peaked when he cried out, "DON'T
TAKE HEAVEN FROM ME!"

He made note that it was the hope of Heaven that

largely brought those black slaves in the Deep South to embrace the Gospel. My black pastor friend was fearful that the preaching and singing about Heaven would be forgotten by the next generation. One can appreciate how this could happen in the black community. The suffering of black people has understandably caused a shift toward emphasizing social justice in our time. That said, the cry, "DON'T TAKE HEAVEN FROM ME!" is a timely reminder that this world is not all there is.

If there has been a neglect of the preaching on Hell in our generation, I suspect that the preaching on Heaven has also been overtaken by life in the here and now. The emphasis has been away from things eternal.

It is the Gospel of Jesus Christ that gets us to Heaven. We are all going to die, and after death comes the final judgment (Heb. 9:27). The question "Where will you spend eternity?" is surely the most important question that can possibly be raised.

I have had the privilege of spending a little time with Billy Graham. I have also spent some moments with his eldest daughter, Gigi. I asked her one day, "Gigi, tell me, what do you think was the secret to your father?"

She did not hesitate to answer. "Daddy grew up singing a little chorus that influenced the whole of his life":

> With eternity's values in view, Lord,
> With eternity's values in view
> May I do each day's work for Jesus
> With eternity's values in view.
>
> —ALFRED B. SMITH (1916–2001)
> "WITH ETERNITY'S VALUES IN VIEW"[1]

I now bring this book to a close. If you have any doubt regarding where you will spend eternity, please pray this prayer—from your heart:

Lord Jesus Christ, I need You. I want You. I know I am a sinner, and I am sorry for my sins. Wash my sins away by Your blood. Thank You for dying on the cross for me. I repent of my sins. I welcome Your Holy Spirit. As best as I know how, I give You my life. Amen.

NOTES

FRONT MATTER

1. C. S. Lewis, *The Problem of Pain* (New York: Mac-Millan, 1962).

FOREWORD

1. "Smith Wigglesworth's 1947 Prophetic Word," Pray for Scotland, accessed August 22, 2017, http://www.prayforscotland.org.uk/smith-wigglesworths-1947-prophetic-word/.

CHAPTER ONE:
REDISCOVERING THE TRUE GOSPEL

1. "Martin Luther," Biography.com, accessed August 24, 2017, https://www.biography.com/people/martin-luther-9389283.
2. "Luther and Protestantism," Boundless.com, accessed August 24, 2017, https://www.boundless.com/world-history/textbooks/boundless-world-history-textbook/the-protestant-reformation-12/protestantism-56/luther-and-protestantism-1034-17635/.
3. Ian Brown, "Some Monkery," The Reformation Room, April 26, 2017, https://www.thereformationroom.com/single-post/2017/04/27/Some-Monkery.
4. Brown, "Some Monkery."

5. "The Life and Work of Martin Luther," Lutheran Resources, accessed August 24, 2017, http://www.lutheran-resources.org/who_was_luther_2.htm.

6. Richard Barcellos, "Remembering Martin Luther: Part II (Luther's Conversion)," Covenant Baptist Theological Seminary, October 30, 2010, https://cbtseminary.org/remembering-martin-luther-part-ii-luthers-conversion/.

7. Claire Ridgway, "Martin Luther by Sarah Bryson," accessed August 24, 2017, https://www.tudorsociety.com/martin-luther-sarah-bryson/.

8. "Lesson 31—The Spread and Impact of the Reformation," accessed August 24, 2017, http://tinyurl.com/y8h3gjrl.

9. "Martin Luther and the 95 Theses," History.com, accessed August 25, 2017, http://www.history.com/topics/martin-luther-and-the-95-theses.

10. Steven Lawson, "Fortress for Truth: Martin Luther," Ligonier Ministries, October 17, 2014, http://www.ligonier.org/blog/fortress-truth-martin-luther/.

11. "Scala Sancta (Holy Stairs)," New Advent, accessed August 24, 2017, http://www.newadvent.org/cathen/13505a.htm.

12. Danika Cooley, *When Lightning Struck! The Story of Martin Luther* (Minneapolis, MN: Fortress Press, 2015), http://tinyurl.com/yczc22fz.

13. Lawson, "Fortress for Truth."

14. James Reston Jr., *Luther's Fortress: Martin Luther and His Reformation Under Siege* (New York: Basic Books, 2015), http://tinyurl.com/yajcndyy.

15. "The Tower Experience," Reformation Theology, accessed August 25, 2017, http://www.reformationtheology.com/2010/05/the_tower_experience_1.php.

16. Scott H. Hendrix, *Martin Luther: Visionary Reformer* (New Haven, CT: Yale University Press, 2015), 220, http://tinyurl.com/yajuvhfl.

17. "Modern History Sourcebook—Martin Luther: The Tower Experience, 1519," Fordham University, accessed August 28, 2017, https://sourcebooks .fordham.edu/mod/1519luther-tower.asp.

18. Donald K. McKim, *The Cambridge Companion to Martin Luther* (Cambridge: Cambridge University Press, 2003), 90, http://tinyurl.com/ycr9r7gd.

19. "Martin Luther and the 95 Theses," History.com.

20. "Ninety-five Theses," *Encyclopaedia Britannica*, accessed August 28, 2017, https://www.britannica .com/event/Ninety-five-Theses.

21. Gene Edward Veith Jr., *A Place to Stand: The Word of God in the Life of Martin Luther* (Nashville, TN: Cumberland House, 2005), 47, http://tinyurl.com /ycfo6pbz.

22. "Ninety-five Theses," *Encyclopaedia Britannica*.

23. "Ninety-five Theses," *Encyclopaedia Britannica*.

24. "Protestant Reformation," Medieval Life and Times, accessed August 29, 2017, http://www.medieval-life -and-times.info/medieval-religion/protestant -reformation.htm.

25. Henry Zecher, "The Bible Translation That Rocked the World," *Christianity Today*, accessed August 29, 2017, http://www.christianitytoday.com/history /issues/issue-34/bible-translation-that-rocked-world .html.

26. "Epistle to Galatians," BiblicalTraining.org, accessed August 29, 2017, https://www.biblicaltraining.org /library/epistle-galatians.

27. "Epistle to Galatians," BiblicalTraining.org.

28. "Martin Luther," PBS, accessed August 29, 2017, http://www.pbs.org/empires/martinluther/char_wife .html.

29. "This Day in History," History.com, accessed August 29, 2017, http://www.history.com/this-day-in-history /martin-luther-excommunicated.

30. "Diet of Worms," *Encyclopaedia Britannica*, accessed August 30, 2017, https://www.britannica .com/event/Diet-of-Worms-Germany-1521.

31. "Diet of Worms," *Encyclopaedia Britannica*.

32. Archie Parrish, ed., *A Simple Way to Pray: The Wisdom of Martin Luther on Prayer* (Okahumpka, FL: Serve International, 2011), https://pcabookstore .com/samples/4764.pdf.

33. Martin Luther, *Luther's Works, 33: Career of the Reformer III* (Minneapolis, MN: Fortress Press, 1957), https://www.goodreads.com/work /quotes/4878257-luther-s-works-33-career-of-the -reformer-iii-luther-s-works. Bracketed statements appear in some sources.

34. Lawrence Cummins, "Martin Luther—Defender of Justice and Seeker of Truth," The Church of Jesus Christ of Latter-Day Saints, October 1984, https:// www.lds.org/friend/1984/10/martin-luther-defender -of-justice-and-seeker-of-truth?lang=eng.

35. Cummins, "Martin Luther."

36. "Martin Luther Quotes," Goodreads, accessed August 30, 2017, https://www.goodreads.com/author /quotes/29874.Martin_Luther.

37. Ray Shelton, "William H. Durham and the Doctrine of Sanctification," December 1, 1973, http://www .apostolicarchives.com/articles/article/8801925/173917 .htm.

38. Joseph Hart, "Come, Ye Sinners, Poor and Needy," public domain.

CHAPTER TWO:
MISUNDERSTANDING THE GOSPEL

1. R. T. Kendall, *Tithing* (Grand Rapids, MI: Zondervan, 1992).

2. Wayne A. Grudem and Gregg Allison, *Systematic Theology/Historical Theology* bundle (New York: HarperCollins, 2015), http://tinyurl.com/yb2nyonr.

3. Grudem and Allison, *Systematic Theology/Historical Theology*.

4. Augustus Toplady, *The Works of Augustus M. Toplady*, vol. 4 (London: William Baynes and Son, 1825), 265, http://tinyurl.com/yavrhjlz.

5. R. T. Kendall and David Rosen, *The Christian and the Pharisee* (Nashville, TN: FaithWords, 2007).

6. *Martyn McGeown*, "The Notion of Preparatory Grace in the Puritans," Covenant Protestant Reformed Church, accessed October 17, 2017, http://www.cprf .co.uk/articles/preparationism.htm#.WeYTuWhSwdU; see also "1636—Hartford," The Society of Colonial Wars in the State of Connecticut, accessed October 17, 2017, http://colonialwarsct.org/1636.htm.

7. Paul Chang-Ha Lim, *In Pursuit of Purity, Unity, and Liberty: Richard Baxter's Puritan Ecclesiology in Its Seventeenth-Century Context* (Leiden, Netherlands: Brill, 2004), 36.

8. R. T. Kendall, *Calvin and English Calvinism to 1649* (Eugene, OR: Wipf & Stock Publishers, 2011).

9. "D. Martyn Lloyd-Jones Quotes," Goodreads, accessed October 17, 2017, https://www.goodreads .com/author/quotes/7810781.D_Martyn_Lloyd_Jones.

10. Thomas F. Torrance, *The Doctrine of Grace in the Apostolic Fathers* (Grand Rapids, MI: Wm. B. Eerdmans Publishing Company, 1960).

11. Torrance, *The Doctrine of Grace in the Apostolic Fathers*.

12. For more on this read John Piper, *The Future of Justification: A Response to N. T. Wright* (Wheaton, IL: Crossway Books, 2007).

CHAPTER THREE:
RECOGNIZING AND AVOIDING THE COUNTERFEIT

1. R. T. Kendall, *The Sermon on the Mount* (Grand Rapids, MI: Chosen Books, 2011).
2. Donald L. Roberts, "John Wycliffe and the Dawn of the Reformation," *Christianity Today*, accessed October 17, 2017, http://www.christianitytoday.com /history/issues/issue-3/john-wycliffe-and-dawn-of -reformation.html.
3. Barry Hoberman, "Translating the Bible," *The Atlantic*, February 1985, https://www.theatlantic.com /past/docs/issues/85feb/transbib.htm.
4. "The Oxford Martyrs: Thomas Cranmer— Archbishop of Canterbury," Continuing Reformation, October 18, 2015, https://continuingreformation .wordpress.com/2015/10/18/the-oxford-martyrs -thomas-cranmer-archbishop-of-canterbury/.
5. Kendall, *Calvin and English Calvinism to 1649*.
6. In communication with the author.

CHAPTER FOUR:
A FALSE TEACHING AT LARGE

1. In communication with the author.
2. "Marcion," New World Encyclopedia, accessed October 17, 2017, http://www.newworldencyclopedia .org/entry/Marcion.
3. In communication with the author.
4. In communication with the author.
5. R. T. Kendall, *Holy Fire* (Lake Mary, FL: Charisma House, 2014).

CHAPTER FIVE:
UNASHAMED OF THE GOSPEL

1. *Strong's Concordance*, s.v. *"euaggelion,"* accessed October 17, 2017, http://biblehub.com/greek/2098 .htm.
2. E. M. Bounds, *Power Through Prayer* (Eastford, CN: Martino Fine Books, rev. 2014), https://www.bible believers.com/em_bounds/em-bounds_ch17.html
3. "Ludwig Feuerbach," Boston Collaborative Encyclopedia of Western Theology, accessed October 18, 2017, http://people.bu.edu/wwildman/bce/feuerbach .htm.
4. L. Agnes Russell, "Protestant Reformation Was Monumental for Modern Christians," Appeal.com, October 17, 2017, http://newtoncountyappeal.com /columns-social/protestant-reformation-was -monumental-modern-christians#sthash.GsqfJAXU .dpbs.
5. Martin Luther, "Preface to the Letter of St. Paul to the Romans," Christian Classics Ethereal Library, accessed October 18, 2017, http://www.ccel.org/l /luther/romans/pref_romans.html.
6. F. F. Bruce, *Romans* (Downers Grove, IL: InterVarsity Press, USA, 1985), 20–21, https://books .google.com/books?id=UTC1CgAAQBAJ&pg.
7. R. T. Kendall, *In Pursuit of His Glory* (Lake Mary, FL: Charisma House, 2004).
8. In communication with the author.

CHAPTER SIX:
THE HEART OF THE GOSPEL

1. Ronald Reagan Quotes," Goodreads, accessed October 18, 2017, https://www.goodreads.com /quotes/29359-there-is-no-limit-to-the-amount-of -good-you.

2. C. H. Spurgeon, *All of Grace*, accessed November 17, 2017, https://www.ccel.org/ccel/spurgeon/grace/files /grace.html.

3. "Fourfold Satisfaction," The Charles Spurgeon Sermon Collection, accessed October 18, 2017, http:// thekingdomcollective.com/spurgeon/sermon/2726/.

4. Francis A. Schaeffer, "Baptism of Infants," ReformedLiterature.com, accessed October 18, 2017, http://www.reformedliterature.com/schaeffer-baptism -of-infants.php?print=on.

5. Johnathan Arnold, "Baptism Is Not About Making a Public Statement," God's Missionary Church, September 13, 2017, http://www.godsmissionarychurch .org/blog/baptism-is-not-about-making-a-public -statement.

CHAPTER SEVEN:
THE FAITH OF CHRIST

1. David Brainerd and Jonathan Edwards, *The Life and Diary of David Brainerd* (Grand Rapids, MI: Baker Book House, 1989).

2. John Wesley, *The Works of the Reverend John Wesley, A.M.* (New York: T. Mason and G. Lane, 1839), 232, https://books.google.com/books?id =g8gOAAAAIAAJ&dq.

3. In communication with the author.

4. John Calvin, *Institutes*, 3.1.1, as quoted in "Calvin: No Salvation Without Sanctification," Mere Orthodoxy, October 25, 2013, https://mereorthodoxy.com /calvin-no-salvation-without-sanctification/.

5. Charles Wesley, "Entered the Holy Place Above," public domain.

CHAPTER EIGHT:
GENUINE, NOT COUNTERFEIT, FAITH

1. *Strong's Concordance*, s.v. *"peitho,"* accessed October 18, 2017, http://biblehub.com/greek/3982.htm.
2. Augustus Toplady, "Rock of Ages," public domain.
3. Matthew Westerholm, "The 'Cream of Creation' and the 'Cream of Faith': The Lord's Supper as a Means of Assurance in Puritan Thought," *Puritan Reformed Journal*, January 2011, http://www.galaxie.com /article/prj03-1-12#GPRJ3A123.
4. Martin Luther, "Martin Luther's Definition of Faith," Internet Christian Library, accessed October 18, 2017, https://www.iclnet.org/pub/resources/text/wittenberg /luther/luther-faith.txt.
5. John Calvin, *John Calvin: Selections From His Writings*, ed. John Dillenberger (New York: Anchor Books, 1975), 401, https://books.google.com/books ?id=C8PQCwAAQBAJ&pg.

CHAPTER NINE:
FAITH AND WORKS

1. In communication with the author.
2. R.T. Kendall, *Justification by Works* (Carlisle, UK: Paternoster, 2001).

CHAPTER TEN:
WHY BE A CHRISTIAN?

1. Jonathan Edwards, "Sinners in the Hands of an Angry God," accessed October 18, 2017, https://www .blueletterbible.org/Comm/edwards_jonathan /Sermons/Sinners.cfm.
2. Billy Graham, *Where I Am: Heaven, Eternity, and Our Life Beyond* (Nashville, TN: Thomas Nelson, 2015).

3. R. T. Kendall, *Total Forgiveness* (Lake Mary, FL: Charisma House, 2007).

CHAPTER ELEVEN:
HELL

1. William Booth, cited in R. T. Kendall, *Unashamed to Bear His Name* (Grand Rapids, MI: Baker Books, 2012).
2. John Newton, "Amazing Grace," public domain.
3. C. S. Lewis, *Letters to Malcolm* (Wilmington, ME: Mariner Books, 2002).
4. Thomas Brooks, *Heaven on Earth* (Edinburgh: Banner of Truth, 1961).
5. C. S. Lewis, *The Problem of Pain* (New York: Mac-Millan, 1962).
6. Wayne Grudem, *Systematic Theology* (Grand Rapids, MI: Zondervan, 1994).
7. Charles Wesley, "Where Shall My Wondering Soul Begin," public domain.
8. R. T. Kendall, *The Parables of Jesus* (Grand Rapids, MI: Chosen Books, 2008).
9. Mary A. Kidder, "Is My Name Written There?," public domain.

CHAPTER TWELVE:
HEAVEN

1. Ira Stanphill, "Mansion Over the Hilltop," public domain.
2. R. T. Kendall, *Prepare Your Heart for the Midnight Cry* (Lake Mary, FL: Charisma House, 2016).
3. Fanny Crosby, "Saved by Grace," public domain.
4. "The Four States of Libertas Naturae," Reformation Theology, May 16, 2006, http://www.reformation theology.com/2006/05/the_four_states_of_libertas _na_1.php.

5. R. T. Kendall, *Worshipping God* (Lake Mary, FL: Charisma House, 2017).

6. John Oatman Jr., "Holy, Holy Is What the Angels Sing," public domain.

7. William W. Walford, "Sweet Hour of Prayer," public domain.

8. R. T. Kendall, *Totally Forgiving God* (Lake Mary, FL: Charisma House, 2012).

9. Albert Edward Brumley, "This World Is Not My Home" (Albert E. Brumley & Sons, 1937, renewed 1965).

10. E. Hewitt, "When We All Get to Heaven," public domain.

11. Esther Kerr Rusthoi, "When We See Christ," (Chicago, IL: Brentwood-Benson Composer Publishing, 1941, renewed 1969).

CONCLUSION

1. Alfred B. Smith, "With Eternity's Values in View" (Chicago, IL: Brentwood-Benson Music Publishing, 1941, renewal 1969).

INDEX

seeker-friendly   35, 41, 125, 127

Septuagint   146

Sermon on the Mount, The   29

Shepard, Thomas   18

Shepherd of Hermas   23

"Sinners in the Hands of an Angry God"   123, 175

Smith, Alfred B.   182

Southern Baptist Theological Seminary   88

Spurgeon, Charles H.   66, 75–76, 107

Stanphill, Ira   158

St. Augustine of Hippo   24, 80, 145, 170

substitution   76

Systematic Theology   139

T

Tada, Joni Eareckson   66

Tertullian   145

Tillich, Paul   89–90

Toplady, Augustus   15, 106

Torrance, Thomas F.   23, 89–90, 93

Total Forgiveness   129

Totally Forgiving God   174

Trevecca Nazarene College   10, 127

Tyndale, William   29–30

U

universalism   xxxii, 91, 140

universal obedience   32

University of Wittenberg   3

W

Walford, William W.   172

Wesley, Charles   95, 142, 172, 176

Wesley, John   55, 87, 175

Where I Am: Heaven, Eternity, and Our Life Beyond   128

Whitefield, George   101–103, 175

Williams, R. T.   9

Wimber, John   xxxiii

Worldwide Church of God   22

Worshipping God   171

Wycliffe, John   29–30

Y

Yeshua   54